PUFFIN BOOKS
B.R. AMBEDKAR

Payal's debut novella, *Wisha Wozzariter*, won the Crossword Book Award 2013 for Children's Writing and is also featured in the *101 Indian Children's Books We Love!* compilation.

Payal finds that stories abound everywhere, sometimes in real life, sometimes in the imagination. She studied English Literature at St Xavier's College, Bombay, and earned a Master of Science degree in Journalism from Northwestern University, Chicago. She worked with *Outlook* in Bombay and *The Japan Times* in Tokyo. Journalism, however, was meant only to be a pit stop, and today Payal is living her dream of being a full-time author.

She lives in Bombay with her husband, Kunal; her two daughters, Keya and Nyla; and their three imaginary friends: Klixa, Pallading and Kiki. She has three exciting children's books lined up for this year: the first of a two-book series about the world's most horrible school; a novel about two unlikely princesses; and this biography for which the great life of B.R. Ambedkar provided ample inspiration.

B.R. AMBEDKAR

SAVIOUR OF
THE MASSES

PAYAL KAPADIA

PUFFIN BOOKS

An imprint of Penguin Random House

PUFFIN BOOKS

USA | Canada | UK | Ireland | Australia
New Zealand | India | South Africa | China | Singapore

Puffin Books is part of the Penguin Random House group of companies
whose addresses can be found at global.penguinrandomhouse.com

Published by Penguin Random House India Pvt. Ltd
4th Floor, Capital Tower 1, MG Road,
Gurugram 122 002, Haryana, India

First published in Puffin by Penguin Books India 2014

Copyright © Payal Kapadia 2014

10 9 8 7 6 5 4 3 2

ISBN 9780143332282

Typeset in Bembo by Eleven Arts, Delhi

Printed at Repro India Limited

www.penguin.co.in

Contents

1   A Train Ride

It was his very first train journey, and the boy could not contain his excitement. He was only nine, and he had never so much as seen a train, let alone been on one. This was the year 1901, and passenger trains had only been recently introduced. A train ride was a big deal indeed, and it was a wonderful stroke of luck that the summer break had begun with one!

The boy's mother had died recently, so the prospect of a summer break was a welcome one. The boy and his older brother had been left in the care of their aunt after their father was called away on work to a place called Koregaon. With the summer holidays around the corner, the father had sent word to the two boys to visit as soon as school closed.

The children sent word back to their father asking him to meet them at the station. In their joyful preparations, no expense was spared—they bought new shirts, new silk dhotis, bright, bejewelled caps and new shoes. The boys waited eagerly, counting the days, one by one, and finally, the day of the great train journey arrived.

It was hot as ever, and as the children clambered into the tonga that would take them to the station, their new clothes itched a little. But they gave this no thought, waving cheerfully to their aunt who sobbed bitterly to see them go. At the station, the boy's elder brother bought the tickets, and then gave the boy and their cousin two annas each to spend as they saw fit. Two whole annas! That was a grand haul, a king's ransom, and the children celebrated their new riches by splurging on bottles of cool lemonade.

Soon enough, the train chugged into the station, and it was every bit as grand as they had imagined it to be. The children climbed in quickly for fear of being left behind. They were to get off at Masur, the closest railway station to Koregaon, where their father was working as a cashier.

The train swallowed up the tracks as it sped forward, the wind tangling the children's hair as villages and fields whizzed by. The hours flew, and it was evening when the children gathered their luggage and got off the train at Masur.

They looked around, expectant, for a familiar face— their father's servant, or better still, their father himself. But there was no one at the station to receive the boys. In but a few minutes, all the other passengers who had got off with them had disappeared.

The children waited. A whole hour passed. The sun was beginning its descent into the evening sky. The early elation of their train trip was turning into a niggling worry.

A man walked up to the children and asked to see their tickets. It was the stationmaster. When the children told him of their plight, he seemed moved. 'What caste do you belong to?' he asked them.

This question might seem odd today, but it was perfectly normal to ask this of someone more than a hundred years ago. In those days, Hindu society was divided into four *varnas*, or castes: Brahmins, Kshatriyas, Vaishyas and Shudras. There was nothing new about these divisions; they went back thousands of years.

In the Vedic period, there was no caste system, or *chatur varna*, as we know it today. In Sanskrit, *varna* literally means colour and *chatur* means four. The *Purush Sukta*, one of the first hymns of the Rig Veda, alludes to four social divisions, when it tells the story of how the world was created. This hymn is dedicated to Purush, a primeval giant. The gods sacrificed this giant, the story goes, and from his body, the world was created. From his mouth were created the Brahmins, his arms, the Kshatriyas, his thighs, the Vaishyas, and from his feet, the Shudras.

The Vedic Aryans divided themselves on the basis of occupation, so people fell into four categories depending upon the work they chose to do. Those who took to books and learning became the Brahmins; those who preferred warfare and governance became the Kshatriyas; traders were known as Vaishyas; and those who served these three classes were termed the Shudras.

But over time, these divisions became watertight, especially after the decline of Buddhism—Buddhism had been the dominant religion for over a thousand years—in 600 CE or 700 CE. You were born into a caste and you could never escape it. This was fine, perhaps, if you were a Brahmin, with all the privileges of money and education. But if you were a Shudra, you were condemned to serve the upper castes. The plight of an Untouchable was still worse. Being an Untouchable was even worse than being a Shudra, because Untouchables fell outside the Hindu fold. They were outcastes, or *a-varna*.

Before his elder brother could stop him, the boy blurted: 'We are Mahars.' The boy's reply might not mean much to us now, but it held great significance for the stationmaster. The Mahars were one of the largest Untouchable castes of India, and in Maharashtra, every village had its Maharwada, or special Mahar quarters. The Mahars were the watchmen of the village, but they also served as porters for travellers, village guides, sweepers of roads, couriers for messages, and collectors of cattle carcasses.

What was it like to be an Untouchable? It was a living death. Untouchables had to eke out a meagre living on the outskirts of villages and towns, sweeping streets, skinning carcasses and tanning hides to make shoes, or worst of all, clearing the urine and excrement of the upper-caste Hindus. It was because the Untouchables had to clear cattle carcasses and human excrement that they were stigmatized and considered impure.

Untouchables existed all over India, only known by different names: *pariahs*, *panchamas*, *atishudras*, *namashudras* and *avarnas*. No high-caste Hindu would touch an Untouchable; even his shadow was considered to be polluting. If a caste Hindu was approaching, an

Untouchable was expected to clear the way for him. It was not uncommon for Untouchables to wear earthen pots around their necks so that their spit would not defile the ground. They also had to tie a broom behind them so that it would sweep away their footprints as they walked.

Untouchables could not draw water from any of the village wells, and they had to drink filthy water wherever they found it. Their children could not attend schools attended by upper-caste Hindu children. Hindu temples were out of bounds to them. Barbers refused to cut their hair; washermen refused to wash their clothes. Upper-caste Hindus led lives full of contradictions. While they were happy to throw sugar to ants or grain to birds, they did not have any kind thoughts to spare for an Untouchable.

The Untouchables had no freedom to decide what to wear, what to eat, or even what domestic animals to rear in their homes. Their rough-hewn clothes told them apart, and they were forced to beg for food at the back doors of high-caste Hindu homes, or to stand outside the doorway of a shop to buy rations.

As soon as the stationmaster heard the boy's answer, his attitude underwent a transformation. The boy was a Mahar, but because he was dressed in fancy clothes, he hadn't been recognized as one. Now his honest reply to the stationmaster had changed everything. The stationmaster's concern for the children gave way to revulsion, and he returned to his room, leaving the children standing there, bewildered and alone.

The stationmaster returned a half-hour later. What were the children going to do, he asked. There were many bullock carts plying for hire outside the station, but the boy's reply had already made its rounds among the drivers. No driver would risk being polluted by carrying Untouchable children in his bullock cart. The children offered to pay double the fare, but they discovered that money was of no use in persuading people to change their beliefs.

Suddenly, the stationmaster seemed to have an idea. 'Can you drive a cart?' he asked the children. The desperate children shouted, 'Yes, we can!' The stationmaster negotiated with the driver of a cart on the children's behalf, and so it turned out that the children would drive the cart themselves and pay the driver double the fare to walk beside the cart.

By now, the sun had set, and the children were anxious to reach Koregaon before it became dark. The driver assured them that it would take no more than three hours to get there. The children set off, reins in hand, the driver walking by their side. A short while later, they came across a trickle of water in the dark, a small river of sorts. The driver told them to stop here for their meal as they would find no water later on. Then he took a portion of the fare that they owed him and went off to eat his own meal, promising to return soon.

The hungry children opened the tiffin box their aunt had packed for them and started eating. They needed water to wash their food down, so one of them went to the trickle of water that ran near the cart. But it was not a small river—far from it. It was nothing more than a sludge of mud, cattle-urine and cow-dung. It stank so much the children could not drink from it.

The children's stomachs were hardly full, but they shut their tiffin box for want of water, and waited for their driver to return. There was no sign of him for a long time, and just when the children feared that they had been abandoned, he reappeared. For a few miles, he walked beside the cart. Then, suddenly, he sprang into the cart, taking the reins himself, as though he were no longer fearful of being polluted by the presence of the Untouchable children. What strange behaviour, the children thought, but they were anxious to get to Koregaon and did not dare to ask him any questions.

Night was falling fast. There were no street lights to illuminate their way. The road was deserted, and the children grew fearful of how alone they were in the gathering darkness. More than three hours had passed, and yet there was no sign of Koregaon. Then a terrifying thought took a hold of them: what if the driver intended to spirit them away to a desolate spot and then kill them for the gold ornaments they were wearing?

'How long until we reach Koregaon?' they asked him repeatedly. But when he did not reply, the children grew even more frightened and started crying. That was when they saw a small light burning in the distance. 'The toll-collector's hut,' said the driver, 'we will rest there for the night.' The relieved children stopped crying. It was midnight when they reached the hut, and the boys were painfully hungry. 'Will we get some water here?' they asked.

'Not if you tell the toll-collector that you are Mahars,' said the driver brusquely. 'Tell him you are Muslims.'

The boy, tired, thirsty and hungry, went to the toll-collector and asked for water. 'We are Muslims,' he said. But his lie did not pay off. 'Do you think I have kept water for you?' asked the cruel toll-collector. 'If you want it, you must go get it from the top of the hill yourself.'

His elder brother's face was expressionless when the boy told him what the toll-collector had said. Perhaps it was all too much to bear. 'Lie down,' he said simply. The cattle had been unyoked, the cart had been placed sloping down on the ground, and the children made their beds inside the cart. Hunger burned inside them. They could not eat because they had no water, and they had no water because they were Untouchables. That indignity hurt more than all the hunger and thirst in the world.

It was not easy to sleep on an empty stomach. After a restless night, the children left for Koregaon at eight the next morning, arriving at their father's home at eleven. Their father was shocked to see them. It turned out that the servant had forgotten to convey the children's message to their father, and he had not known of their date of arrival.

Perhaps some of the terror and the humiliation the children had experienced melted away with the sudden joy of being reunited with their father, but the boy remembered this train ride for the rest of his life. It was not as if he was new to the stigma of being untouchable, but for the first time, he found himself thinking hard about what it really meant.

The boy, this Untouchable child from a small rural town, was none other than Bhimrao Ramji Ambedkar. He rose from the poorest, the most oppressed class of society to become the architect of the Constitution of India, and yet he never forgot the burning shame of untouchability. He fought bitterly against the caste system and led a lifelong crusade to win for the rights of the Untouchables.

And where it all started, like all great stories that begin small, was a single train ride and a night spent thirsty, frightened and Untouchable.

Who were the Untouchables?

The first mention of untouchability is found in the Chandyoga Upanishad: 'Those who are of delightful conduct will quickly attain a delightful womb—a Brahman womb, a Kshatriya womb or a Vaishya womb. But those who here are of foul conduct will quickly attain a foul womb—a dog's womb, a pig's womb or a Candala womb.' 'Candala' stands for the Chandalas, or the Untouchables, those who were given the task of disposing of dead bodies. Even in the philosophical texts of the Upanishads, Untouchables were considered no better than pigs or dogs!

What is the Vedic period?

The Vedic age or the Vedic period refers to the time when the most ancient scriptures of the Hindus, the Vedas, were written. The exact dates for the Vedic period can only be guessed at, but it is considered that the oldest Veda, the Rig Veda, was composed somewhere between the 17th century BCE and the 11th century BCE. There are four main Vedas, or ancient Sanskrit texts of the Vedic period: the Rig Veda, the Sama Veda, the Yajur Veda and the Atharva Veda.

2 ✎ Lessons at School

Perhaps it was always clear that B.R. Ambedkar, known affectionately in his childhood as Bhim or Bhiva, was destined for greatness. He was born in Mhow, a small garrison town in Madhya Pradesh, on 14 April 1891, the last of fourteen children. Before his birth, a prophecy was made by a great-uncle of his who had renounced the world and become a sanyasi. He predicted that Bhim's father, Ramji Sakpal, and his mother, Bhimabai, would have a son who would leave his mark on history. The great-uncle could not have been more right.

In his earliest years, Bhim did not directly feel the insult of being Untouchable. To begin with, his father dropped the family name, Sakpal, as it was obviously low-caste. Instead, he used the name of his ancestral village, Ambavade, as was the practice at the time in Maharashtra, changing the family name to Ambavadekar ('kar' meaning 'belonging to').

The family also had greater access to education and resources than usual because of Bhim's father's job as a subedar-major in charge of a military school. Bhim's paternal grandfather, Maloji Sakpal, was a retired military man. On his mother's side, her father and her six uncles were all subedar-majors in the army.

Among the Mahars, joining the military was an old tradition. The Mahars were a huge presence in the British army, so they enjoyed the advantages of cantonment life, such as compulsory schooling and living in military quarters, instead of dark, unsanitary shanties. Because of the peculiar combination of being educated but poor, the Mahars were more politically conscious and their leaders were acutely aware of their rights. It is no surprise then that a leader like Bhim arose from the ranks of the Mahars.

Bhim was barely two years old when his father retired from military service. The family moved from Mhow to Dapoli in the Konkan region. In Dapoli, Bhim first went to school. His father did not stay long at Dapoli and soon secured a job in the Public Works Department at Satara.

Soon after their arrival in Satara, the family faced a tragic blow—Bhim's mother died. Bhim was barely six years old at the time. Of Bhimabai's fourteen children, only three sons and two daughters had survived. Her death was a devastating blow for them all. Balaram was the eldest, Anandrao was the second, then came two daughters, Manjula and Tulsi, and finally, Bhim, the youngest. In the absence of a mother to raise the boys, the two daughters, both married, took turns looking after their brothers. Ramji's sister, Mirabai, also helped bring up the children. Bhim was her favourite because he was the youngest.

It was in Satara that Bhim first experienced caste discrimination. In school, he was forced to sit apart from the other students, squatting on a piece of gunny cloth that he had to carry home with him at the end of the day because the school cleaner would not touch it.

The teachers would not so much as touch his notebooks. Some of them hesitated to ask him questions or assign him a poem for recitation because they feared that he would pollute them if he spoke to them directly. When they were thirsty, the other children could go to the school tap, open it and drink. But when Bhim was thirsty, he had to wait for the school peon to pour water into his cupped hands from above. If the peon was not at school the boy had to go thirsty. He put it in his own words quite well: 'No peon, no water.'

There were isolated acts of kindness in his life, though. There was a Brahmin teacher at Bhim's school called Mahadev Ambedkar, who, it is said, was a most infrequent visitor to his own classroom. He had another day-job as an accountant at a tobacco shop nearby. During class hours, he would sneak off to the shop, leaving the class in the care of a grown-up Muslim student. But when the school inspectors made their annual visits, Ambedkar showed his sympathy for his students by standing behind the inspector and giving out the answers to arithmetical problems!

Ambedkar took a liking to Bhim. Every day, he shared some of his own lunch with Bhim, dropping it into his outstretched hands. In the school register, he changed Bhim's name from Ambavadekar to Ambedkar, giving the Untouchable boy his own name. In later years, Bhim would remember his teacher fondly, although he was not as much a good teacher as he was a good person.

Bhim's greatest teacher, though, was his father. Ramji Sakpal was a teacher by training, and he served as headmaster in the military school at Mhow for fourteen years. He was a well-read man, reciting the epics of the Ramayana and the Mahabharata to his children. He also sang them the spiritual songs of great Marathi poet-saints like Tukaram and Mukteshwar. The family followed the Kabir school of thought, like many other Untouchable families at the time. Typically, Kabir followers worshipped Lord Krishna or Lord Rama, but most significantly, they did not believe in the rigidity of the caste system as Kabir had clearly condemned it.

In the military quarters at Mhow, life followed strict military rules. Every household put out its lights at a fixed time. Ramji Sakpal would stay up late into the night, crooning softly to his children with the doors and windows tightly shut so no sound carried outside. Constant recitals of these songs gave the children a certain command of Marathi from an early age.

Bhim's father also studied English and liked arithmetic, and introduced his sons to both subjects. Discipline and religion were very important to him. Prayers were offered twice a day, and he expected his children to attend without fail and to participate in singing the hymns. Any disobedience on this front was met with unforgiving sternness.

Bhim also inherited from his father a deep interest in the welfare of society. Ramji Sakpal was a friend and admirer of Jyotirao Phule, the founder of the anti-Brahmin movement in Maharashtra. In 1892, the government of India issued orders banning the recruitment of Mahars into the Indian army, mainly because the Hindu soldiers who came from other castes objected to sharing their barracks with Untouchables.

Gopalbaba Walangkar, a former soldier, led the first protest against this order. Walangkar's is a prominent name in Dalit history because he fought hard to secure the rights of the Untouchables much before Bhim emerged as a leader. Though Walangkar's petition did not find any support at the time because people were too fearful to speak out against the injustice, several other petitions were filed later.

Bhim's father also took an active role in the protest. He approached M.G. Ranade, another noted reformist, to draft a petition to the government to retract its orders. Years later, Bhim would come across his father's old papers, and it would make him proud to see his father so concerned with the fate of the Untouchable community—and to realize that he was truly his father's son.

Who were the Mahars?

It is held by some that the Mahars were the original inhabitants of Maharashtra, which, they say, was a 'Mahar-rashtra', or 'land of the Mahars'. The Mahars were Maharashtra's poorest Untouchables. In spite of their extreme poverty, the Mahars were certainly not the worst off among the Untouchables. They did not specialize in any craft, so they were the first to leave the villages and experience modern city life.

Who are Kabir, Tukaram and Mukteshwar?

Kabir, Tukaram and Mukteshwar were mystic poets and saints associated with the Bhakti movement. The Bhakti movement originated in Tamil Nadu and then spread northwards during the late middle ages. This was an unorthodox movement, emphasizing absolute devotion to God or Bhakti, and setting aside caste distinctions and Brahmanical rituals. The progressive Bhakti movement revived Hinduism at a time when the Islamic rulers of north India were pressuring their Hindu subjects to convert to Islam, but it would be wrong to call it a Hindu movement. One of its leading saints, Kabir, was raised in a Muslim family, and even in Tukaram's famous songs, there is no mention of the word 'Hindu'.

3   A Man of Maharashtra

The story of any human being cannot be fully understood without looking closely at where he comes from. Bhim's rise to greatness had plenty to do with his iron will, his vast intellect and his public-spiritedness, and these values were his father's legacy to him.

But Bhim was also heir to a strong regional tradition. His ideas of equality and justice found their early roots in the anti-Brahmin movements that emerged in Maharashtra from the mid-19th century onwards, and in Western patterns of thought brought in by British rule.

What was Bhim's home, Maharashtra, like before the British arrived? Under the rule of Chhatrapati Shivaji Maharaj, social relations at the village level were organized according to the *balutedari* system, also known as *bara balutedar*, or twelve *balutedars*. These balutedars provided hereditary services to the village. There was a caste system even among the balutedars and they were by no means equal. The Patil (or moneylender) and the Kulkarni (or village accountant) typically came from the higher castes and had dominant roles. The astrologers came from the Brahmin caste, but the other *balutedars* were all from the lower castes. They included, among others, the Sonas (or goldsmiths), Lohars (or ironsmiths), the Mangs (or ropemakers) and the Chambhars (or leatherworkers).

After the death of Shahu, Shivaji's grandson, the Peshwas usurped the throne. The Peshwas were Brahmins, and they were bitterly resented by the Marathas, who belonged primarily to the peasant classes, although a few Maratha clans claimed to be Kshatriyas. This tension between the Peshwas and the Marathas points to a conflict between Brahmins and non-Brahmins very early in the history of Maharashtra.

The last Peshwa surrendered his power in 1818 after being defeated in war by the British East India Company. Through the 19th century, British colonialism began to undermine the caste system. The Brahmins were already accustomed to education and found it easy to enter the educational system that the British had set up to train local administrators. The superior education of the Brahmins gave them an upper hand when it came to bagging the best jobs in the British bureaucracy.

The British-run schools were closed to the Untouchables because upper-caste pupils opposed the idea of studying along with them. At best, Untouchable children could study sitting on the school verandah. The government had set up special schools for Untouchables, but these schools were too few in number to provide a proper education to large numbers of Untouchables.

In 1813, Christian missions were allowed to settle in India. At first, the missionaries focused on providing education, but soon enough, they were conducting public debates to promote Christianity as a better alternative to Hinduism. They used the printed word to spread their ideas, publishing pamphlets, books and newspapers. They challenged the idea of idol worship; they professed that there was only one God; and they denounced the caste system.

Their egalitarian ideas began to take hold in the minds of lower-caste Hindus who had long suffered under the caste system. The Brahmins' greater access to both education and employment aroused hostility among them. This paved the way for the birth of the anti–Brahmin movement.

In the face of this steady assault against Hinduism, some Brahmins became convinced of the need to reform themselves and their beliefs in order to counter the impact of the missionaries. This led to the parallel emergence of reform movements dominated by the upper castes, although none of them argued for the abolition of the caste system itself.

The anti-Brahmin movement, on the other hand, was much bolder in its scope, denouncing the caste system altogether. It is closely linked to the life of a man called Jyotirao Phule, who was the founder of India's first low-caste organization, the Satyashodhak Samaj. Bhim was born within a year of Phule's death and was deeply influenced by him. He later dedicated one of his books to the memory of Phule.

Phule was a Mali, born into the caste of gardeners. He was very fortunate to receive an education at the Scottish Mission in Pune, and his schooling brought him in touch with Western philosophy and thought. He was very drawn to the figure of Christ, who stands for equality and brotherhood. In fact, Christian values had a strong impact on Mahars till the early 20th century, with some of them converting to Christianity. Phule opposed the caste system and described Brahmins as oppressors—either as greedy moneylenders or as priests who took advantage of the blind faith of the poor.

One day, Bhim's political career would echo Phule's own. From Phule, Bhim learnt to distrust upper-caste reform movements and to believe that the Untouchables must liberate themselves on their own. Phule distanced himself from the Indian National Congress, founded in 1885 in Bombay, and regarded it as a Brahmin pressure group. Like his predecessor, Phule, Bhim's relationship with the Congress would be rocky at best.

When Bhim first appeared on the political scene in Maharashtra, a new social and political consciousness was emerging among the lower-castes. They were eager for change and hungry for good leadership. This presented a unique opportunity to Bhim to prove himself. This is where his education and his intelligence were of great use to him. If he had not doggedly pursued an education, there might have been no story to tell.

Who were the Peshwas?

The Peshwas served as prime ministers to the Marathas. The title of Peshwa was first created by Chhatrapati Shivaji Maharaj to oversee the administration of his massive empire, with its capital in Raigad. The Maratha Empire flourished from 1674 to 1818, and at its peak, it covered much of South Asia. During Shivaji's rule, the Marathas fought a twenty-seven-year war with the Mughals, the longest war in Indian history, and they emerged victorious. After the death of Shivaji's grandson, Shahu, the Peshwas became the de facto rulers of the Maratha Empire, which reached its zenith during their reign.

What reform movements arose within upper-caste Hinduism?

Christianity influenced the Prarthana Samaj, or the Society of Prayer. Its founders wanted to replace the idol worship of Hinduism with the belief in one God. The most well-known member of the Prarthana Samaj was M.G. Ranade. He believed that man and God should have a direct connection, and he wanted Hinduism to rid itself of Brahmins, or priests.

The Arya Samaj was founded in 1875 in Bombay by Swami Dayanand Saraswati. He, too, like Ranade, denounced idol worship and the caste system, but he argued that these faults were only modern-day corruptions of an ancient Vedic model.

4   A New Love for Books

As a young boy, Bhim did not take to his studies easily and had no interest in examinations, in spite of his father's educative influence. It wasn't that surprising, really, when you think of all the shame and ridicule that he had to endure at school. However, in the face of such cruelty, Bhim stood fearless and defiant.

Once, a classmate dared him to walk to school without an umbrella. Not one to let a challenge go, Bhim marched to school in the torrential rain, arriving soaked to the bone. The class teacher took pity on him and asked his son to take Bhim to their home, and to give him a hot bath and a piece of cloth to wear. Bhim was thrilled at the prospect of getting a day off from school, but his joy quickly melted into disappointment when he was called back to the classroom, to spend the rest of the day doing his lessons half-naked.

Little known to Bhim, his aversion to studies was about to undergo a dramatic change. Something would happen to transform Bhim from a truant boy into a promising student. And then there would be no looking back.

When Bhim was less than ten years old, his father remarried. Bhim hated the idea of another woman replacing his mother. Feeling angry and defiant, he decided that it was time to stop depending upon his father. Bhim had heard his sisters tell stories of boys from Satara finding jobs in the mills of Bombay, and this filled him with hope. But how was he to go to Bombay without any money of his own?

So he hatched a plan to steal money from his aunt, who slept next to him on the floor every night. His aunt would tuck her purse safely into her waist belt, and for three stressful nights, Bhim tried to reach it without waking her up. On the fourth night, at long last, he got his hands on the purse, only to find, to his utter disappointment, that it contained only half an anna in it—certainly not enough to buy a trip to Bombay!

The guilt of being a thief was so intense that Bhim decided to give up his shameful plan. Instead, he resolved to study hard so that he could clear his examinations and do something on his own merit. From a shirker he grew into a dedicated pupil, so much so that his teachers now told his father to give him the best education or opportunities possible.

In 1904, when Bhim was thirteen, the family moved to Bombay. Home was now a small room in Dabak Chawl at Lower Parel. Bhim and his brothers were admitted to Maratha High School. By now, Bhim was better at English than most of his classmates and he had discovered the wonderful world of reading. He had an unquenchable thirst for new books, but you can only imagine that books were not easy to come by for an Untouchable boy living in a modest one-room tenement.

But Bhim's father indulged this desire of his, taking small loans from his married daughters and even leaving the jewellery he had gifted them on their wedding days at the pawn shop. He would redeem their jewellery at the end of the month when his own pension payments came through. He was very keen on his son becoming a scholar, and he oversaw Bhim's studies with a stern eye and a firm hand.

After a few months, Bhim was sent to Elphinstone High School. He learnt early on that if you want to succeed at something, you have to give it your best. He had no desk of his own and no money for a private tutor, yet he made no excuses and studied hard. It was hard to find any quiet time in this tiny home for a boy to study in peace, but Bhim's father devised a plan.

Before his exams, Bhim would go to bed early, with a grindstone near his head and a goat asleep beside him, because the single room he lived in was a shed, kitchen and study all in one. His father would stay up until two in the morning, only to awaken his son to study and then sleep in his place. Bhim would study till the early hours of morning in the faint light of a kerosene lamp. After a short nap, he would bathe and go to school.

Bhim's new school had as many humiliations in store for him as all the schools he had attended earlier. Once, a teacher called upon Bhim to solve a sum on the blackboard. The caste Hindu children, who kept their lunch boxes behind the blackboard, were furious. Before Bhim could do as the teacher had told him to, the other children had rushed to the blackboard and flung their tiffin boxes aside, because they did not want Bhim to touch the blackboard and pollute their food. Another time, a teacher tried to advise Bhim to give up his studies, saying that it was useless for him to spend time on education. Anger welling up inside him, Bhim told the teacher to keep his opinions to himself!

There were many little dreams and ambitions that he had to sacrifice because he was an Untouchable boy. He was very keen to study Sanskrit, but Sanskrit was the language of the Vedas and no Untouchable was allowed to read or listen to the Vedas. Instead, he was forced to take Persian. In later years, Bhim would study Sanskrit himself and become a self-taught scholar in the language.

Bhim had no friends as a student and most of his teachers had nothing to say to him. He spent his free time reading in a nearby garden. Here, the principal of Wilson High School, Krishna Arjunrao Keluskar, noticed the studious boy and often loaned him books to read.

It is strange how the people we seem to meet by accident often affect our lives in profound ways. It was Keluskar who helped Bhim secure admission in Elphinstone College after he passed his matriculation exams in 1907. It was also Keluskar who gifted Bhim a copy of his book, *Bhagwan Gautam Buddhache Charitra* (*Life of Gautam Buddha*). Buddha's teachings would move Bhim deeply as he grew older.

In 1905, at the age of fourteen, Bhim was married to Ramabai, who was only nine years old! Of course, it seems unimaginable now that such young children could be married, but this was a normal practice at that time. Bhim's wedding took place in a rather strange venue: the open shed of Bombay's Byculla Market. At night, after the day's haggling and purchasing had been done, the bridegroom and his family took shelter in one corner of the shed, the bride and her family in another. Narrow, open drains of filthy water flowed beneath their feet, but they were unmindful of the squalor. They turned the little stone platforms of the market into makeshift benches for the guests to sit on, and the marketplace was transformed into a marriage hall.

Right after the wedding, Bhim plunged into his college studies again. In 1907, when he cleared the Standard Ten exam, it was an incredible achievement. At that time, only one out of every hundred Mahars could read and write! When his father ran out of money to pay for his college education, Keluskar came to Bhim's rescue. He called upon the Maharaja of Baroda, Sayajirao Gaikwad III, a progressive ruler who had announced only a few days earlier that he would help any worthy Untouchable in the pursuit of higher studies.

The Maharaja met Bhim and was so impressed that he granted him a scholarship. Bhim's friendship with Keluskar had proved to be a fortuitous one! Around this time, the family moved into another chawl at Parel. There, they had two rooms opposite each other. One was used as a study and the other for household purposes. As the final exams drew closer, Bhim concentrated all his energy on studying hard, with his father seated outside, keeping vigil.

In 1912, Bhim passed his BA exams. His oldest son, Yashwant, was born the same year. During this time, the British government clamped down on the rights of Indian citizens. The Indian Press Act of 1910 muzzled the press. Public gatherings and discussions were banned, and anyone who protested was branded a traitor.

Bal Gangadhar Tilak, a powerful nationalist leader, had been deported by the British and sent to Mandalay, in Burma, to suffer six years in exile. Veer Savarkar, another Indian freedom fighter and revolutionary, was arrested in 1910 and sentenced to prison in the Andaman and Nicobar Islands. Maharashtra was in the grip of severe political unrest and this must have had an impact on the mind of young Bhim.

Later, in a historic thesis of his, titled *The Evolution of Provincial Finance in British India*, Bhim indicted the British government for its repressive measures in no uncertain terms.

After his graduation, Bhim decided to take up a service position in the state of Baroda state to express his gratitude to the Maharaja. His father dissuaded him from going, warning him that he would face far more discrimination in Gujarat than he had ever faced in Bombay. But often, you will agree, we tend to think that we know better than our parents. Bhim was no different at that age. He was adamant, and even quarrelled with his father to go to Baroda.

But when he reached Baroda in January 1913, he found to his total dismay that his father was right. No one would give an Untouchable lodging and he had to eat in the Untouchable quarters of the city. At work, he was shifted around from one place to the next as no department wanted him.

Fifteen days later, he received a telegram from Bombay: his father was terribly sick. He reached home only in time to see his father die. For Bhim, it was an indescribable loss, and he cried bitterly for no one had done as much for him as his father had. With the death of his father, he had lost his greatest ally and friend.

Heartbroken, Bhim resolved not to return to Baroda. He made his case to the Maharaja, and the kind ruler of Baroda offered him a scholarship to study at Columbia University in the United States of America. In return, Bhim agreed to serve the Baroda State for ten years on the completion of his studies.

It was an opportunity of the most unbelievable kind. An Untouchable was to venture abroad to study at one of the world's finest universities. What a long way Bhim had come! From a boy who wanted to run away to the mills of Bombay, he was now an eminently qualified young man about to embark on an educational journey with the best minds of his generation. He was the living, breathing proof of the fact that education can liberate you and transform you, no matter where you come from.

What is a chawl?

Chawl is an Anglicized version of the Marathi word *chaal*, which is typically a four- or five-storeyed building with a long common corridor on each floor, and many *kholis* (or one-room homes) leading off it. Every floor has a common set of latrines. Chawls were instrumental in the growth of Bombay. As the city's cotton mills boomed, there was a demand for cheap labour. Chawls were built in the 19th and early 20th centuries to accommodate the huge flood of rural migrant labourers who came to Bombay looking for work. Their residents were a hardy, resourceful lot who found creative ways to solve their common problems of food and childcare. The common corridors of the chawl became bustling social hubs. The shared experience of eking out a living in Bombay brought the residents together, so that chawls became a sort of community, with a unique life and colour.

5   Unaccustomed Freedom

In July 1913, Bhim embraced a whole new world. New York was an exciting experience for him. Untouchability was of little or no significance to both the Indians and the Americans there. It was like the doors of a prison had been thrown open. For the first time in his life, Bhim enjoyed the company of his fellow students. He could think and speak freely, he could go where he liked, he was accepted as an equal. Nothing could be a greater revelation to young Bhim. In the early days he watched plays, played badminton and learned how to ice skate.

He began to appreciate how his education had become the key to his freedom. The thought was a powerful one—a person could, through hard work and study, overcome his situation. This way of thinking would deeply influence how Bhim led his community in the years to come—by preaching self-help and self-respect as the tools of emancipation.

For the first week, Bhim stayed at the university dormitory, but most of the dishes contained beef and Bhim could not eat them. He soon shifted to another dormitory where he forged a lasting friendship with a Parsi student called Naval Bhathena.

There were so many new things to learn and discover, from eating with a fork and knife to exploring the dynamic city of New York. But Bhim was not the carefree son of a rich man. He had a family of ten people back at home, struggling to survive on the meagre earnings of Bhim's brother Balram, who worked as a common labourer.

Soon enough, Bhim regretted all the frivolity of his early days in New York, and with a renewed sense of purpose, turned to his studies. He had an insatiable thirst for knowledge, the sort of intellectual curiosity that can never be quenched. He spent all his free time reading anything he could get his hands on at the library, or hunting for deals at second-hand bookstores. He purchased about 2000 old books, using his money for little else. He had a hearty appetite, yet he ate sparingly, saving a part of his stipend to send home to his family every month.

He took up political science, anthropology, sociology, economics and moral philosophy, studying eighteen hours a day, and was determined to learn as much as he could. He was a student of America's most famous philosopher, John Dewey, who taught him to believe in the power of democracy to bring about social equality.

Bhimrao was also inspired by Booker T. Washington, a black leader who promoted education as the tool for African American freedom. His favourite teacher, though, was Edwin R.A. Seligman, an economist. It was Seligman who guided Bhim towards earning his MA in 1915 and writing his PhD dissertation in 1916.

Studying at Columbia University might have been enough for Bhim to rest on his laurels and go home. But, instead, aiming higher still, he turned his attention to London. He set off the same year to study advanced economics at the London School of Economics and to train for Law at Gray's Inn, one of the four associations of barristers and judges in London. His Baroda scholarship had expired, and Bhim appealed to the Maharaja for an extension.

He was given one year to wind up his studies, after which he would be forced to return to India. What an unbearable interruption this must have felt like for a young man in a hurry to make the most of every opportunity given to him! There was so much to learn and so little time! But Bhim promised himself that he would return once he had earned some money to pay his way. He got permission from London University to resume his studies within four years.

It was the time of World War I, and as Bhim sailed back to India in 1918, a steamer was torpedoed in the Mediterranean Sea. His family assumed that Bhim was on that ill-fated steamer and mourned their loss, only to discover to their joy that he was travelling on another ship, and the steamer that was sunk carried only his luggage. Bhim, however, wasn't as overjoyed as the rest of his family. He shed tears for his lost bags as they contained many of his treasured books.

Back in India, the British government was in crisis. World War I was a watershed in the relations between India and Britain. The news of Indian soldiers fighting and dying side-by-side with British soldiers travelled far and wide. It also intensified the demands for self-government among nationalist Indians.

Beset by war losses on one side and by the clamour for home rule in India on the other, Edwin Montagu, the Secretary of State for India, declared in August 1917 that the British would gradually try to promote self-government in India. Montagu visited India to study public opinion on the subject, and for the first time, the Untouchables were also able to present their case. However, Bhim was not on the political scene at the time. He was busy making preparations to set off for Baroda to take up his new post as military secretary to the Maharaja.

After the openness of America and England, Bhim had forgotten what it was like to be an Untouchable. Baroda was a harsh reminder that nothing had changed in India. He had to pay his own passage to Baroda, and being short of funds, he used the money he had been awarded as damages for his torpedoed luggage.

No one came to the station to receive him and guide him in the new city. No Hindu hotel or hostel would accept a Mahar. He had friends in Baroda who had studied with him in America, but they were not Untouchables like him. No high-caste Hindu friend would want to welcome an Untouchable guest into his home, so Bhim stood at the railway station, undecided and lost, quite like the boy at Masur station many years ago.

Finally, he found boarding at a Parsi hostel, pretending to belong to the community. Bhim was quite alone there, and he dreaded returning to such a dark bat-ridden dungeon at night. There were no electric lights, not even oil lamps, only a small hurricane lamp whose light could not extend more than a few inches. He felt enraged, even saddened, that even after being educated and employed, this dungeon was his only shelter in an unfriendly, narrow-minded town. His sister's son came from Bombay, bringing his remaining luggage. When the boy saw how his uncle was living, he cried so loudly he had to be sent back immediately.

At work, things were as oppressive. Brahmin colleagues insulted him to his face and peons threw papers on his desk in the rudest fashion to avoid making contact with him. Things finally came to a head when a group of angry Parsis discovered his true identity and forced their way into the boarding house to beat him up. At that time, Bhim valued a roof over his head more than his very life, and he implored the Parsis to give him some time to find new accommodation. But he discovered that they were not different from high-caste Hindus. They were adamant and told him to be off.

Shaken to tears, he thought of where else to go. Baroda was a large town, and yet there was no room in it for an Untouchable like him. He had two friends there, a high-caste Hindu and an Indian Christian. But the Hindu said, 'If you come to my house, my servants will leave,' and the Christian said he could not take a decision without consulting his wife, who was out of town. It was a tactful answer because, in truth, the

Christian friend's wife was orthodox and would not like the idea of an Untouchable in her home.

Defeated and disillusioned, Bhim took the train to Bombay that night. He spent the evening in a public garden, thinking of how even something as basic as shelter was out of the reach of an Untouchable, no matter how educated he might be; of how an Untouchable could not count on having friends from other castes; of how an Untouchable would always cause problems for himself and for others, no matter where he went.

Who was Edwin Montagu?

Montagu was Secretary of State for India between 1917 and 1922. He was primarily responsible for the Montagu–Chelmsford Reforms. These reforms were laid out in the Montagu–Chelmsford Report of 1918 with the purpose of gradually introducing self-governing institutions to India. They were put into the Government of India Act of 1919, which was meant to expand the participation of Indians in the governance of India. It committed the British to the task of eventually granting India the status of a dominion. Many countries that were formerly ruled by the British Empire were later given dominion status, which means that they were under British sovereignty, at least in name, but they were otherwise independent. Several of them, like India, became republics later.

6   A Second Chance Abroad

Returning to Bombay, Bhim struggled to earn a livelihood. There was so much prejudice against Untouchables that this was no easy thing. No one would trust an Untouchable lawyer with a case. The solicitors would not have any business dealings with him.

At last Bhim heard of a teaching vacancy at Sydenham College. He accepted it in 1918 with a view to earning his way back to London. He realized, very quickly, that as an Untouchable professor, he did not enjoy any credibility with his students. What could a Mahar possibly teach them, they thought. But in time, the students came to realize that their thinking had been erroneous. They were won over by Bhim's insightful teaching methods and his breadth of knowledge. It was not as easy to win over the other teachers, who objected to Bhim drinking water from the tumbler reserved for professors.

At about the same time, another reform-minded ruler, Shahu Maharaj of Kolhapur, was also taking interest in the removal of untouchability. Over the years, he would develop a close relationship with Bhim, exchanging warm letters with him.

Shahu Maharaj helped Bhim to start a bimonthly paper called *Mook Nayak* in 1920. Here, Bhim's voice was heard for the first time as a leader of the Untouchables. India was the home of inequality, he wrote, like a multi-storeyed tower with no ladder. In another article, he wrote that if the Brahmins were justified in their opposition to British rule, the Depressed Classes, as the Untouchables were known in British times, were far more justified in their opposition to the rule of the Brahmins.

In March of the same year, Bhim presided over a conference of the Untouchables in Mangaon in the state of Kolhapur. This conference was sponsored by Shahu Maharaj, and after the conference, he invited Bhim to join him for dinner. Later, Bhim requested Shahu Maharaj to preside over another conference for the Depressed Classes in Nagpur. Here, Bhim told his community about his distrust of any caste Hindu organization working for the betterment of the Untouchables. He felt that any movement to uplift the Untouchables should originate from within the community.

At the end of the Nagpur conference, Bhim attempted to unite the Depressed Classes by hosting a dinner for them. While eighteen subcastes of the Mahar community attended the dinner, Bhim was not able to persuade all the other Untouchables to come. It is ironic that while Bhim was fighting for the abolition of caste, the Untouchables were still very much divided among themselves by the same system they were being told to destroy.

During these early years, Bhim did not enter the political arena, except to speak on behalf of the Untouchables before British committees. It was his reasoning that while political rights were very important for the emancipation of the Untouchables, social reform was equally pressing.

Viceroy Lord Chelmsford and Secretary of State Montagu were recommending reforms for British India. In a follow-up to the Montford reforms, as they were known, the Southborough Committee was set up to tour India and survey the opinions of Indians on the idea of voting. The aim was to revise the qualification criteria for voting and to allow more Indians to vote during the assembly elections. Bhim was called before the committee because he was the only Untouchable in the Bombay Presidency with a graduate degree. He demanded separate electorates and reserved seats for the Depressed Classes.

Bhim was concerned that the Depressed Classes would not get true representation. This is because India follows a system known as First-Past-the-Post or the FPTP system. For the purpose of elections, the country is divided into constituencies, but only one candidate is elected from each constituency, the candidate with the largest number of votes, or the candidate first past the post. It is like a running race where there can only be a single winner, the first runner to cross the finish line.

This means that even if there are Jews, Christians, Sikhs, Dalits, Hindus and Muslims living together in one constituency, only the candidate selected by majority voters will go to Parliament. In India, in most constituencies, the majority voters are Hindu. And so if a Hindu candidate typically bags the most votes, minority voters will never be able to field their own candidate.

In Bhim's time, it was assumed that the two major religious communities in India were the Hindus and the Muslims, and the British were busy appeasing both of these groups. But Bhim felt that there was one more division that was often overlooked but was very significant—that between the caste Hindus and the Untouchables. He feared that in an FPTP system, only a caste-Hindu candidate would get the most votes, and that the Untouchables would be shut out. That didn't seem very fair to Bhim.

To find a solution to the problem, Bhim first looked at the system of separate electorates, a system that had been used by the Muslims. By this method, only Untouchables could vote for Untouchable candidates.

But this method was not free of drawbacks. If a minority group were to get its own quota of representation and nothing else, the rest of the legislative assembly would owe no allegiance to that group. In other words, separate electorates are divisive in nature and do not achieve the aim of integrating the minority group into the mainstream.

On the other hand, by the reserved seats method, a certain number of legislative seats would be demarcated for Untouchables. But there was further danger here. High-caste Hindus, who were in a majority, could elect the Untouchable of their choice, one who would do their bidding in the legislature in exchange for a seat.

Bhim argued that a multi-seat constituency, in which more than one candidate was elected from each constituency, would be a fairer form of representation. Seats would be allotted proportionally to different parties based on the number of votes they had won. Although Bhim did not call this the system of Proportional Representation—it is known as such today—he had the foresight to imagine such a system could exist.

Bhim finally had to drop his demand for separate electorates and to settle for reserved seats. As a result, the current electoral system has never been questioned and rethought as it should have been. The outcome is that even though the Constitution provides for reserved seats for Dalits today, they are not adequately represented because the majority parties often sponsor their own Dalit candidates to capture a Dalit seat.

★★★

Bhim was paid well as a professor, yet he continued to live frugally, in the same two rooms of the Parel chawl where he had once studied for his BA degree. He gave a fixed portion of his monthly pay to his wife Ramabai to be directed towards household expenses. It was not an easy life at any point, and both poverty and ill health were constant companions. Ramabai gave birth to her second son, Ramesh, when Bhim was in America, but the child died in infancy. Their third child, too, later passed away in childhood.

Of all the children Ramabai had borne, only her firstborn, Yeshwant, survived, and his frail health caused his mother tremendous worry. Yet she lived as thriftily as she could, keeping away from Bhim's study, not wanting to distract him with concerns about the family.

Where there is a will, there is a way—it was this belief that kept Bhim going. At long last, after drawing on his savings, borrowing money from his friend Naval Bhathena and receiving some help from the Maharaja of Kolhapur, Bhim returned to London in 1920. Ramabai was left to her own devices again.

Life in London was not easy for Bhim either. It took a lot of resolve to live on little money, but Bhim was not to be discouraged by hardship. He had seen enough of it all his life. He would rise at 6 a.m., wolf down the meagre breakfast that his landlady provided him, and then set off for the library at the British Museum. Here he would sit, from opening to closing, chased out by the watchman in the evening as the last to leave, his pockets bulging with the notes he had written down. After a short walk in the evening, he would return to a sparse dinner at the boarding house, then study into the wee hours, sustained by a cup of tea and a couple of papads (a gift from an Indian acquaintance) that he would fry for himself.

He had no money to spare for the cinema, for the theatre, for lavish dinners, and sometimes even for a bus ride home. He walked endlessly through the mighty city of London, exhausting one library after another in his quest for knowledge. In all those arduous years, Bhim did not forget the plight of the Depressed Classes back home. He took great interest in the running of *Mook Nayak*. He was also concerned about the education of his son and his nephew and had a tutor engaged to look after them.

Here, in London, Bhim also developed a close relationship with his landlady's daughter, Fanny Fitzgerald. She took notes for him on various subjects, possibly lent him money and took care of his books for him when he returned to India. It cannot be said for certain what Bhim's feelings for her were, but she was evidently in love with him.

In 1921, Bhim earned his Master's degree in economics, and in 1922, he submitted his doctoral thesis to the University of London. Around the same time, he was called to the Bar. Yet, yearning to learn more, Bhim went to Germany to study at Bonn University. He had hardly been there a few months when his professor called him back to London. His thesis, he was told, had offended his British examiners because of its anti-imperialist tone. Bhim was asked to rewrite it without changing its conclusions.

This was not the first time that Bhim's controversial ideas had caused a stir in the academic circles of London. Only a few days before, he had read a paper at the Students' Union titled *Responsibilities of a Representative Government in India*. It had triggered heated debate, which had to be called to an end on the grounds that the topic being discussed was too revolutionary for a student group.

By this time, Bhim's money had run out and he could not imagine staying back in London to rewrite his thesis. He returned to Bombay in April 1923, and submitted the same thesis a few days later. The examiners accepted it and he was overjoyed to be awarded a doctorate. Bhim became the first Indian to receive a Doctor of Science degree from the London School of

Economics. What a crowning achievement it was! Instead of using his difficult circumstances as an excuse for failure, Bhim had overcome them, through sheer hard work and perseverance. He had kept his promise to himself.

Shudras, Untouchables, Depressed Classes, Dalits, Scheduled Castes—what do all these terms mean?

Simply put, Shudras were the fourth *varna*. They were heavily disadvantaged, but they were not as badly off as the Untouchables, or outcastes, who were outside the folds of the caste system, or *a-varna*. 'Depressed Classes' was a term used during British rule. Dalits, which literally means 'ground down,' is probably the most preferred term today. Jyotirao Phule first used the term in the 19th century. The Dalits are referred to as 'Scheduled Castes' in the Constitution.

Who was the Maharaja of Kolhapur?

Shahu IV, also known as Rajarshi Shahuji Chhatrapati and Chhatrapati Shahuji Maharaja, was the ruler of the Indian princely state of Kolhapur between 1894 and 1922. He turned anti-Brahmin after the Brahmins of Kolhapur refused to grant Kshatriya status to the Marathas, barring them from all Vedic rites, including family ceremonies. Shahu IV did a lot to advance the lower castes in his state, making education free for all and building hostels for lower-caste students.

7   A New Political Class Emerges

Bhim returned from London to an India in the throes of social turmoil. The fall of the tsars in Russia and the rise of Marxism had fuelled a working-class awakening. The Depressed Classes were beginning to assert themselves. A South Africa-returned lawyer named Mohandas Karamchand Gandhi was infusing fresh blood into the nationalist movement spearheaded by the Congress Party. Gandhi made the removal of untouchability an integral part of the Congress manifesto.

Bhim wanted to begin practising law so he registered at the Bombay High Court. Caste Hindus were reluctant to approach him with cases, so he earned money by teaching law part-time and by working as an examiner for Bombay University.

It was at this point that Bhim became more actively involved in politics. The Depressed Classes were beginning to grow restless for social change. People of the Untouchable community routinely gathered at his house. In March 1924, he set up the Bahishkrit Hitkarini Sabha, an organization to promote education and culture among the Depressed Classes, to advance their economic condition and to represent their grievances. It was also the first time that the Untouchables, in their use of the word 'bahishkrit', had tried to arrive at an acceptable name for their own community.

In 1926, Bhim was appointed to the Legislative Council of the Bombay Presidency. This was the beginning of his long, impressive career as a legislator.

His leadership skills were put to the test when the small town of Mahad became the seat of the first great mass struggle of the Untouchables in 1927. Here, the municipality had passed a resolution allowing Untouchables to draw water from the Chavdar Tank. But the caste Hindus were against this resolution and hence, no Untouchable dared to drink water from the tank. On 19 and 20 March, a conference was staged at Mahad to assert the Untouchables' right to draw water from the tank. More than 10,000 Untouchables gathered at Bhim's call. 'We are going to the tank to assert that we, too, are human beings like others,' he thundered.

Led by Bhim, the Untouchables marched to the tank and drank its water. Soon after, a band of angry upper-caste people set upon the Untouchable delegation to teach them a lesson and beat them. Many of the Untouchables were wounded, and others had to find shelter in Muslim houses. The Untouchables were enraged by the brutal attack, and it was tempting to think of revenge. But Bhim held them back, preaching self-restraint and non-violence. Their protest, he insisted, should be a peaceful one.

The Mahad conference made headlines for months. Some newspapers criticized the Depressed Classes for making such a brazen move, others condemned the shameful behaviour of the caste Hindus. Either way, the first public attempt of the Untouchables to assert their civic rights became a historic event. The Untouchables were now bristling from the indignities they had suffered at Mahad. They awoke to a new sense of self-respect and gave up skinning carcasses or begging for crumbs. They also realized that they had a right to drink water from public watercourses, just like anyone else. It was this day, 19 March, that the Depressed Classes began to observe as their day of independence.

In August the same year, the Mahad Municipality withdrew its resolution to declare Chavdar Tank open to the Untouchables. The tank was purified by pouring into it 108 pots of a mixture of cow-dung and cow-urine. It seems incredible that for the traditional Hindus, cow excrement was more pure than the hands of a thirsty Untouchable!

In response Bhim announced a second satyagraha, or a peaceful protest. The town of Mahad began to stir again. Police were posted at the Chavdar Tank. Untouchables began to pour in from everywhere, singing songs and shouting slogans. On 24 December, Bhim addressed a huge gathering of 15,000 people of his community. Standing in front of the crowd, he declared that India must adopt the principle that all men are born equal.

Beasts and birds can drink this water, he told his followers in a memorable speech, but Untouchables are barred because caste Hindus do not want them to be considered as social equals. The Mahad satyagraha is not a march for water, he said, it is a march for equality.

Drinking water from the tank would not make any great change in their lives, said Bhim, but it would help reconstruct society on the lines of the same principles that had once guided the French Revolution—liberty, equality and fraternity.

He declared war on the Manusmriti, the ancient scriptural text of the orthodox Hindus. The Manusmriti, followed zealously by devout Hindus, forbade the Shudras from reading or listening to the Vedas. That night, copies of the Manusmriti were placed on a pyre and burned by Untouchables, just as Indian nationalists had burned foreign-made cloth to challenge colonial exploitation. The Chavdar Tank battle eventually turned out to be a long one, and Bhim fought the case in the Lower Civil Courts for nearly ten years.

But just as Bhim was beginning to prove himself a leader to reckon with, tragedy struck his family yet again. In 1926, Bhim's son Rajaratna died as a baby, of double pneumonia. Bhim had loved him dearly, spending happy hours playing with him. Before the birth of Rajaratna, a girl, Indu, had been born, but she too, had died in her infancy. Rajaratna's death was a cruel blow from which Bhim never fully recovered. He was so devastated that he would not let go of his son's body, and for days, could not bring himself to enter the room where his son had breathed his last. In a letter to a friend, he wrote, 'With his passing away life to me is a garden full of weeds.'

The following year, Bhim's older brother, Balram, passed away and with his death, Bhim inherited the responsibility of looking after Balram's wife and son. Now his meagre finances would have to suffice for not just his own family, but also his brother's. It seemed like the situation couldn't get any worse.

For all the education that Bhim had sought and found in the Western world, Bhim's life was also a lesson in the reality of being poor in India. Sickness and early death—these were the things that most Indians experienced at the time. Bhim's mother died early; so did his elder brother and four of Bhim's five children. Poor sanitation, malnutrition, lack of medical care and disease made life a cruel journey for the poor. This was a truth in Bhim's time, and it holds true even today.

In 1929, Bhim tasted the utter humiliation of being an Untouchable once again. On behalf of the Bombay government, he was touring the province to investigate the grievances of the Untouchables. His travels took him to Chalisgaon station, where he was met by the Untouchables of the area. They entreated him to spend the night in their homes. Overwhelmed by their love, he accepted the invitation.

The Maharwada was but walking distance from the station, across a river. There were many tongas for hire outside the station, and yet it took an hour for a tonga to be arranged. Soon after Bhim boarded the tonga, they almost collided with a motor car.

Bhim was taken aback by the tonga driver's lack of experience, but before he could remark on it, they approached the culvert on the river. The culvert was at right angles to the road, and the tonga had to take a sharp turn. Near the very first side stone of the culvert, the horse bolted and turned instead of going straight. The wheel struck the side stone so forcefully, Bhim was thrown into the air by the impact, landing hard on the stones of the culvert. The horse and carriage fell into the river.

Bhim had fractured his leg, and after a little while, he was carried to the Maharwada. No one told him at the time, but the truth was that the tongas outside the station had refused to carry an Untouchable. Embarrassed, Bhim's followers did not want their leader to go on foot. Finally, a tonga driver had agreed to rent out his tonga to the Mahars, as long as they drove it themselves. The Mahars ended up risking Bhim's safety for the sake of his dignity. The incident forced Bhim to swallow a bitter truth once again—that despite being a qualified lawyer, he would always be considered inferior by anyone who wasn't an Untouchable.

Who was Karl Marx?
Karl Heinrich Marx was many things—a writer, a philosopher, a historian and a journalist, among others. But he is best known for developing the theory of Marxism. Marxism is the collective name for Marx's theories about society, economics and politics, and it still influences the world today. What does the theory say? It's very complicated, but to put it simply, Marx said

that society progressed through class struggle. He was against capitalism, which he called the rule of the upper classes for their own benefit. He predicted that capitalism would eventually wear down and give way to socialism, or the rule of the working classes. He predicted that the world would eventually move to a classless society, or communism. Although his predictions have not quite come true, his Marxist ideas had a major hold on the former Soviet Union and modern-day China.

What is satyagraha?

The word 'satyagraha' is a combination of two Sanskrit words, satya (or truth) and graha (or holding on to). Satyagraha, meaning 'the force of truth', is an idea that was developed by Gandhi to fight for Indian independence. It is a form of non-violent, or civil, resistance. Gandhi believed that violence would only beget violence, so the aim of satyagraha was to eliminate injustice without harming the wrongdoer. The idea of satyagraha was so effective and moving, it influenced many justice struggles across the world, including Nelson Mandela's struggle against apartheid in South Africa and Martin Luther King Jr's struggle for black rights in the United States.

What does the Manusmriti say about the lower castes?

A Shudra's role, according to the Manusmriti, is to serve Brahmins so that he may attain a higher caste in his next birth. If a Shudra curses an upper-caste man, he shall have his tongue cut out. If he uses contemptuous words to refer to an upper-caste person, he shall have a red-hot iron nail thrust into his mouth. If a Shudra tries to teach a Brahmin his duty, hot oil will be poured into his mouth and ears. If he tries to seat himself next to an upper-caste person, his hip will be branded. Shudras should not be allowed to acquire any wealth. They should wear the clothes of the dead, adorn themselves with only ornaments of black iron, and eat from broken dishes.

The Manusmriti was also probably the foundation of our patriarchal system. It said that a woman should never be independent: as a child, she should be under the control of her father; as an adult, under the control of her husband; and as a widow, under the control of her son.

8 The Knights of the Round Table

Soon after the Mahad protest, Bhim found himself at the centre of a new controversy. The Act of 1919—the Montford Reforms—was only valid for ten years. So in 1928, the British set up the Simon Commission—after its chairman, a great parliamentarian called Sir John Simon—to come up with constitutional reforms for India. The commission visited India to consult representatives of different social groups, but the Congress boycotted the commission as it had no Indian members. Its arrival was greeted with black flags and banners that said: 'Go back, Simon!'

Instead, the Congress formed the Nehru Committee to draft its own constitution for free India. The Congress version reached out to all minorities, including the Muslims, Sikhs, Christians, Parsis and Anglo-Indians. However, it ignored the Depressed Classes and made no provisions to protect them. This made Bhim sceptical of the Congress's commitment to safeguard the rights of the Depressed Classes. It was his view that the Untouchables needed certain constitutional guarantees if they were ever to be integrated into the mainstream of Indian society.

In 1929, Bhim made the difficult decision to cooperate with the all-British Simon Commission. He appeared before the commission and was instantly labelled a British stooge and a traitor by other national leaders. Nothing could have been further from the truth. Bhim was as patriotic as any of our other freedom fighters, but for him, the interests of the Untouchables took precedence over everything else—even independence for India. He understood that cooperating with the British was key to winning political rights for his community. It is likely that Bhim expected the British to be more egalitarian in their outlook than high-caste Hindus.

Bhim submitted a memorandum on behalf of the Bahishkrit Hitkarini Sabha, arguing for a seat quota for Untouchables rather than separate electorates. The memorandum demanded twenty-two seats in the 140-seat Bombay Assembly to be reserved for Untouchables and also for voting rights for all the Untouchables. The Commission finally granted reserved seats for the Depressed Classes, but these were just empty words on paper because the Congress had taken no part in the drafting of the Commission's report. To end the deadlock, the first Round Table Conference was held in London in 1930.

The Round Table Conference was a historic event. For the first time, British and Indian statesmen and rulers met in one place, around one table, to discuss the future government of India. Bhim made a demand for self-government, and once again asked for reserved seats for the Depressed Classes. He argued passionately for the setting up of an Indian republic, in which political power was also shared with the Untouchables. 'We feel that nobody can remove our grievances as well as we can,' he said. No conclusion was reached at the conference because the Congress Party boycotted it, but Bhim's visit to London was far from fruitless.

He grabbed every opportunity to speak to the foreign press, writing for various publications and addressing meetings to publicize the humiliation and the injustice that India's Untouchables had been subjected to for centuries. For the first time, the Western world woke up to the fact that the predicament of the Untouchables of India was even worse than that of the black community in America.

The conference came to an end in January 1931, and by March the same year, Viceroy Lord Irwin had signed a pact with Congress leaders. This pact ended the Civil Disobedience Movement and permitted, among other things, the peaceful picketing of foreign cloth shops, the release of all political prisoners (except those found guilty of violence) and the free collection or manufacture of salt by persons living near the coast. Most importantly, it paved the way for Mahatma Gandhi's attendance at the Second Round Table Conference in September. This conference would pit Gandhi against Bhim in a historic confrontation, with each claiming that he was the rightful representative of the Untouchables.

At Round Two, Bhim was selected to sit on the Federal Structure Committee, which was to play a crucial role in the drafting of a new constitution for India. There was uncertainty about whether Gandhi would attend the second session. However, on 6 August 1931, Gandhi wrote to Bhim, asking for a meeting. A week later, Bhim went to meet Gandhi at his home at Mani Bhavan in Bombay. Bhim was shown into a room where he found Gandhi eating fruits and talking with his partymen. Bhim and his colleagues bowed to Gandhi, and then sat on a blanket on the floor, waiting for Gandhi to finish.

Finally, Gandhi turned to Bhim, only to ask him why he had so many complaints against both the Congress and him. 'I have always been concerned with the question of the Untouchables,' said Gandhi, 'and I fought to make the removal of untouchability a major plank of the Congress manifesto.' He added that the Congress had spent twenty lakhs to uplift the Untouchables and wondered why that was not enough to appease Bhim.

Bhim countered that Congress spending was a superficial measure and that the party was not sincere about removing untouchability. Every member of the Congress Party, Bhim argued, should have to employ Untouchables in their home, or provide shelter to an Untouchable student, or dine with an Untouchable. But opposing untouchability was not considered a condition for membership to the Congress Party. Bhim went on to express his distrust in the Congress Party and in the Mahatma. He bristled with anger at being labelled a traitor by the Congress.

'Gandhiji, I have no homeland,' he said, his face flushed.

When Gandhi disagreed, Bhim continued, 'How can I call this land my own homeland and this religion my own when we are treated worse than cats and dogs, wherein we cannot get water to drink?' Then, Bhim asked him the most important question of all. The first Round Table session had recommended adequate representation for the Depressed Classes.

'What is your opinion?' Bhim asked.

'I am against the political separation of the Untouchables from the Hindus,' replied Gandhi. 'That would be absolutely suicidal.'

This response set Gandhi and Bhim on a collision course that would last their entire lifetimes. For Bhim, the Untouchables were already separate from the caste Hindus. Being ruled by the caste Hindus was an unbearable thought.

At the second session of the Round Table conference, the confrontation continued. Gandhi and Bhim both sat on the Minorities Committee, which discussed what sort of political representation the Muslims and the Depressed Classes would enjoy in a new India. Gandhi opposed Bhim's demand for separate electorates for the Depressed Classes, arguing that separate electorates would fragment the Hindu community. Any hopes that Gandhi and Bhim might see eye-to-eye ended then and there.

The second session wound up inconclusively, and finally the president of the Minorities Committee, Ramsay MacDonald, said that he would come up with a method of his own to end the impasse.

9   Two Leaders, Two Visions

It is a sad fact of history that Gandhi and Bhim, two great leaders, both of whom wanted to free the country from British rule, had deep-seated differences over how to help the Depressed Classes find a place in independent India. Gandhi's approach was more like that of a kindly old uncle, seeking to protect the Untouchables from social persecution. Bhim dismissed the notion that the Untouchables were so helpless that they needed to be protected by high-caste Hindus. He believed strongly in self-help and self-empowerment.

Gandhi was deeply attached to *varnashrama dharma*, or an idealized version of the caste system, a sort of caste without hierarchy. He contested Bhim's view that the Untouchables were demeaned because they had to clear the excrement of others. Gandhi talked of the dignity of all labour and insisted that every resident of his ashram in Ahmedabad should clean toilets. He also talked a lot about *swadharma*, that children should follow their fathers' professions. To Bhim, this was a most unfair idea, as he could not imagine how any man would want to become a scavenger just because his father had done the same sort of work before him!

Gandhi's vision for India was conservative, and he refused to endorse inter-caste marriage, or even the notion of people from different castes eating and drinking together. To be fair, Gandhi's views changed over the years, and he did eventually accept the idea of inter-caste marriage, but he never challenged the notion of caste as a form of social organization. Bhim, on the other hand, felt that the caste system was the root of all Hindu evils and should be destroyed.

Gandhi had a romanticized view of village life, where people had few needs and worked harmoniously in occupations that had been traditionally assigned to them. For Bhim, villages were cesspools of caste tyranny. An urbanized, industrialized society, hated by Gandhians, was a path for social equality for the Untouchables.

At the root of Gandhi and Bhim's differences were two very divergent ways of looking at the Indian nation. Gandhi assumed that India was already a nation and he made a Hindu identity the basis for national identity. It is interesting that when the Depressed Classes adopted Gandhi's strategy of non-violent satyagraha to fight caste oppression, they did not gain Gandhi's support. Satyagraha, according to Gandhi, could not be used by one Hindu to fight another. In other words, he assumed that the Depressed Classes were as much a part of Hinduism as caste Hindus.

But were they really Hindus? Bhim argued that if the lower castes and the upper castes belonged to the same religion, they must have the same rights. If not, there was no place in the Hindu fold for an Untouchable.

Bhim recognized that India was not a nation, but a nation-in-the-making, full of feuding castes and sub-castes. There could be no political identity for India without social equality.

Although the independence of India was necessary for the Depressed Classes to be liberated, Bhim was more concerned with the kind of nation that would be created by the Independence struggle than with the struggle itself. If India was a nation in which equality had no meaning, was it a nation worth making?

It was not an easy thing to oppose Gandhi, and Bhim had to pay a heavy price for doing so. Gandhi had become the beloved Mahatma of the people because of his simplicity and his peace-loving ways. Bhim's thundering voice and his ferocity of purpose simply didn't appear as sympathetic as Gandhi's gentle demeanour. People started talking badly of Bhim, about how he was rude and uncivilized to oppose some of Gandhi's views. Orthodox Hindus feared that he would become the destroyer of Hinduism.

Things came to a head on 16 August 1932, when the British government decided to end the deadlock by announcing what was known as Ramsay MacDonald's Communal Award. It gave separate electorates to the Muslims, the Sikhs, the Christians and the Depressed Classes.

Gandhi opposed it vehemently, going on an indefinite fast unto death in September. Gandhi was in Yerwada Jail at the time, from where he sent a message to the British. He said that he would resist with his life the separation of the Untouchable Hindus from the caste Hindus.

Gandhi's fast was not a fair response to the Award. He had signed a written agreement that allowed the British prime minister to arbitrate a final solution to the communal problem. He should have honoured his word. But with the announcement of his fast, there was shock and confusion in Hindu circles. The Hindus were afraid that their hero would lose his life fasting against the Communal Award.

Bhim was angered by the fast. He felt that Gandhi was using emotional blackmail to get his own way. Sure enough, there was a tremendous outpouring of emotion from all over India, and a furious campaign was launched against Bhim, labelling him a monster and a traitor.

Bhim stood firm and adamant in the face of all this opposition. 'To save Gandhi's life, I would not be a party to any proposals that would be against the interest of my community,' he said.

His strong, cutting words didn't win him any friends. He received death threats, and passers-by on the street cast him angry looks. There was mounting pressure on Bhim to renegotiate the terms of the Communal Award and save Gandhi's life. If Gandhi were to die, Bhim rightly feared, India would never forgive the Untouchables.

In but a few days, Gandhi's health took a turn for the worse. He was too weak to even sit up. His son, Devdas, went to Bhim teary-eyed, begging for a resolution. Bhim was faced with a great dilemma. On the one hand was the life of India's most beloved leader, and on the other, the future of his community. Defeated, Bhim signed the Poona Pact with Gandhi on 24 September 1932, establishing a system of reserved seats for the Untouchables but setting aside the principle of separate electorates.

With the Poona Pact, both sides had to compromise. The caste Hindus had to grant 148 seats to the Depressed Classes in the Legislative Council, almost double of what the Depressed Classes had been promised in the Communal Award. But the Depressed Classes lost the advantage of having separate electorates. Nobody could fail to recognize now that Bhim was the undisputed leader of the Depressed Classes. But in the face of Gandhi's fasting tactics, even he was rendered helpless.

Three days after he broke fast, Gandhi set up the All India Anti-Untouchability League and went on a campaign to promote the interests of the Untouchables. This led to a reconciliation of sorts between Gandhi and Bhim, but sadly, the closeness between the two was short-lived. Differences quickly arose on how the League should function.

The League was dominated by upper-caste Hindus, and although Bhim visited Gandhi in prison to suggest a stronger presence of Untouchables in the League, his recommendations were ignored. The League focused its efforts on fostering values like temperance and cooperation among Untouchables and fighting for their right to enter temples. But for Bhim, temple entry was not the answer to Dalit problems. He wanted the League to focus on social change by fighting for the Dalits' access to water, and their right to go to schools and use other village amenities.

Bhim and the other Dalit representatives soon resigned from the League, which was renamed the Harijan Sevak Sangh. It continued to work for Untouchables in a patronizing manner. Incidentally, the word 'Harijan' gained currency after it was used by Gandhi as the title of a newspaper he published from Yerwada Jail in 1933.

Differences also arose between Bhim and the Congress over other issues. At the end of 1932, some upper-caste Congressmen sought to introduce a bill abolishing untouchability, but Bhim faulted the bill because it did not condemn untouchability as a sin. He argued that it was not enough to abolish untouchability; it was the caste system that had to be eradicated.

'There will be outcastes as long as there are castes,' he wrote.

Finally, for the Untouchables, the Poona Pact was a terrible let-down. It took away any hope they might have had of becoming a political force. It shaped the 1935 Government of India Act, and the reserved seats granted by the Act did not give the Untouchables the sort of representation that was proportional to their demographic weight. Even though the Untouchables were a populous class, they were given only seven seats out of 156 in the Council of State (the Upper House of Parliament), nineteen out of 250 in the Central Assembly (Lower House) and 151 seats out of 1585 in the various provincial legislatures.

Later, in 1945, Bhim published a book called *What Congress and Gandhi have Done to the Untouchables*. It was a scathing attack on Gandhi and the Congress Party. It argued that the Congress's work to uplift Untouchables was driven by the desire to prevent the Untouchables from having a separate political identity of their own.

It must be said that Gandhi had his own limitations. He was perhaps the only Indian politician to make the abolition of untouchability central to the freedom movement, but he also had to appease the orthodox Hindus who dominated the Congress Party and believed he was breaking down social constructs too fast.

Bhim thought just the opposite. He felt Gandhi was pushing social change too slowly, and gradually Bhim moved closer to the British. His fears were very real: that foreign rulers who were indifferent to caste were about to be replaced by upper-caste Hindus who dominated the Congress Party. Would Indian Independence spell a new form of oppression for the Depressed Classes?

What is the Civil Disobedience Movement?

On 12 March 1930, Gandhi inaugurated the Civil Disobedience Movement by conducting the historic Dandi Salt March to oppose British salt laws. The British had imposed heavy taxes on Indian salt in order to favour imported British salt, which was of an inferior quality. The production of Indian salt was gradually outlawed. Even though fine salt had been produced in India for centuries, the commodity became unaffordable during the British Raj. It became almost a luxury to sprinkle salt in your food.

To oppose this injustice, Gandhi, along with an entourage of seventy-nine ashramites, marched from his Sabarmati Ashram, near Ahmedabad, to the coastal village of Dandi, 390 kms away, on the shores of the Arabian Sea. On 6 April 1930, Gandhi violated the Salt Law by picking up a fistful of sand and salt on the seashore. The satyagrahis manually made salt on the shores of Dandi.

The Dandi Salt March had an immense impact on the entire nation. Each and every corner of the country was gripped by the feeling of nationalism. There were reports of satyagrahas from all over the country. Besides the breaking of the salt laws, the Civil Disobedience Movement involved the picketing of shops selling foreign goods and liquor, the burning of foreign textiles and a refusal to pay taxes. Public officers stayed home from work, students from school. Perturbed by the growing popularity of the movement, the British government imprisoned Gandhi and Jawaharlal Nehru. But the movement was a resounding success in involving the masses in the freedom struggle.

10   An Outcaste among Muslims

Fighting for the rights of the Depressed Classes was an all-consuming mission. Bhim often said that he had drowned his own identity, his own needs and wants, in this crusade for equality for his community. Bhim had precious little time for his family or himself. His health began to suffer—his eyesight deteriorated and, he was worried that he would lose his vision completely. No disease or hardship frightened him as much as the thought of losing his sight, because if he were to go blind, he would not be able to read. And for Bhim, a life without books was not a life worth living.

In 1934, he was appointed part-time professor at the Government Law College. A man of his education should have been nothing less than the principal of the college, but it was a difficult, prejudiced time. Bhim's achievements went unrecognized because of the caste he belonged to. He only became principal on 1 June 1935.

It was a constant battle, but Bhim did not let these matters dampen his spirits. He was preoccupied with a new dream, of building a beautiful bungalow in Bombay to house a library of books. He bought books on architecture and studied the subject, building the house, even tearing parts of it down if they didn't please him. Finally, Bhim and Ramabai moved into the house, which was named Rajagriha.

Rajagriha was a high point in their lives. Bhim and Ramabai had seen some terrible times together, including the deaths of four of their children. You might recall all the sacrifices Ramabai made while Bhim was in England and America, pursuing a higher education. She scrounged to make ends meet, raising her children in extreme poverty, and was always careful not to trouble Bhim with her problems.

It could not have been easy for her, being a single mother while her husband was away for long periods of time, staying up long nights waiting for him to come home and worrying about his safety. Ramabai often blamed Bhim's colleagues for burdening him with so much responsibility and putting his life in danger. Once, in an emotional outburst, she insisted on accompanying Bhim to a conference rather than waiting at home for him to return. Bhim dismissed her fears as nonsense, but of course, there was nothing irrational about them.

Ramabai was very ill at this time, but Bhim could not tear himself away from his work to tend to her more closely. Once, he managed to take her away for a change of air to Dharwar, but there was no change in her condition. She began to waste away, her cheeks shrinking, her eyes losing their sparkle.

She nursed a deep desire to make a religious pilgrimage to Pandharpur, like almost every devout Hindu in those days. But this desire of hers was to suffer the fate of all her other wishes, and would remain unfulfilled. As an Untouchable, she would have had to stand at a distance from the temple, offering her prayers from afar. This was unacceptable for a proud man like Bhim and he discouraged her from going. Instead of that Pandharpur where you cannot worship your God as an equal, we will create another, more equal Pandharpur, he said.

On 27 May 1935, Ramabai passed away. Bhim was present at her deathbed. Almost 10,000 people, across all sections of society, attended her funeral. On his return from the cremation, Bhim kept to his room, crying bitterly and inconsolably. It is said that behind every successful man, there is a woman. This is certainly true for Bhim and Ramabai. Everything Bhim did was large and grand: he fought for Dalit rights, and he eventually wrote the Indian Constitution. Ramabai's contribution was seemingly more modest and traditional—raising Bhim's children and running his home—but without her working behind the scenes, Bhim might never have grown to become a leader of the Untouchables.

If you look at the lives of great people anywhere, you will find that there are other individuals, not as great or as well-known, who helped them achieve greatness. In Bhim's life, his father and his wife were those people.

★★★

In 1934, there is another story about Bhim and one more bitter experience of untouchability to be recounted. A group of Bhim's co-workers invited him on a trip to visit the Buddhist caves at Ellora. Desperately in need of a vacation, he was excited about the prospect of going sightseeing for the very first time.

It was common knowledge that Untouchables were met with revulsion wherever they went. So the busload of thirty-odd Untouchables decided not to make their travel plans public, but to move about incognito as far as was possible. On their way to Ellora, this party of Untouchable tourists had decided to make a stop at Daulatabad because the fort there was an ancient historical monument and a major tourist attraction.

The Untouchable community in Daulatabad had been informed of Bhim's arrival, and they waited eagerly for him at the entrance of the town. They pressed Bhim to have some tea and refreshments first, but he was keen to see the fort before nightfall. Bhim and his colleagues proceeded to the fort, with the receiving party soon to follow them.

It was the holy month of Ramzan, and Daulatabad was primarily a Muslim area. Outside the majestic fort was a tank of water, full to the brim. The dusty and weary travellers decided to wash their arms, legs and faces here before carrying on through the large gates, guarded by armed soldiers.

They had just started inquiring from the guard about the procedure for entering the fort, when an old Muslim man with a white, flowing beard came up from behind, shouting, 'The Dheds have polluted the tank!'

Soon all the Muslims who were nearby, both young and old, started abusing the Untouchable party and shouting, 'They have become arrogant!' and 'They must be taught a lesson.'

The tourists pleaded with the Muslims to hold their anger. 'We are outsiders and did not know your local customs,' they said. But the Muslims' anger would not be appeased. They turned on the local Untouchables.

'Why did you not tell these outsiders that this tank could not be used by outsiders?' they said. 'You are to blame for this!'

The local Untouchables had only just caught up and protested that they had not foreseen that something of this sort would happen. But the Muslims continued to shower the choicest abuse on Bhim and his group. It was not easy for Bhim's party to restrain themselves when so many insults were raining down upon them. But at the same time, they did not want to be provoked. A fight could very quickly turn into a riot, and lives would be lost for nothing.

A young Muslim in the group insisted, repeatedly, that people should conform to their religion. What did he mean by that? He meant that Untouchables should know their place and drink water only from a public tank. By now, Bhim had grown impatient and he could not hold his silence anymore.

'Is that what your religion teaches?' he asked angrily. 'Would you prevent an Untouchable from taking water from this tank if he became a Muslim?'

These questions silenced the Muslims. Bhim then turned to the guard and said: 'Can we get into the fort or not? If we can't, we don't want to stay.'

The guard asked Bhim to write his name on a piece of paper. Then he took the note inside to his Superintendent. A short while later, he returned to say that the Untouchable tourists could enter the fort as long as they promised not to touch any water inside the fort. An armed guard was to accompany them to make sure of this.

The incident brought back old and terrible memories for Bhim, of being homeless and alone in Baroda, of waiting as a boy for his father to arrive at Koregaon. It seemed that no matter how much he achieved, discrimination and prejudice would pursue him wherever he went. It was enough to crush his spirit, but as a leader of the Untouchables, he realized, perhaps, that giving up the fight would never be an option.

What are the Ellora Caves

The Ellora Caves are located twenty-nine kilometres north of Aurangabad in Maharashtra and are a UNESCO World Heritage Site. The thirty-four caves were built between the 5th and 10th century CE and are Buddhist, Hindu and Jain temples, mathas, and viharas carved out of the Charanandri hills' vertical face. The Ellora caves are a wonderful testament to the religious harmony which was prevalent during this time in Indian history.

11   A Place beyond Hinduism

The year was 1935. For Bhim, it marked a decade-long struggle, fighting for his community to be accepted into mainstream Hindu society. Everything was a battle, from the right to drink water out of public tanks to the right to receive an education, or the right to enter a Hindu temple. Hinduism appeared most unwelcoming, and it seemed that there was no place in the Hindu fold for an Untouchable and nor would there ever be.

The Mahad struggle over the right of the Untouchables to drink water from the Chavdar Tank had caused Bhim great anguish. The case was being heard in the Mahad court, and as a lawyer, Bhim had to make frequent visits to Mahad. One such trip took place during the monsoons. Heavy rains had caused flooding, and Bhim's car was forced to stop on the way for two days. Bhim found himself in the middle of nowhere, with no Untouchable locality in sight. No one else would give him shelter or food.

The experience caused him so much pain that he returned and shut himself in his room and would not come out. He had laboured so hard to reform Hinduism, to make a place within it for the Untouchables, but now all his efforts seemed hopeless.

It was possibly at this point that he realized that the struggle to reform Hinduism was a dead end. The thought of renouncing Hinduism completely seized his mind. Perhaps, he hoped, this would close one chapter in his life and open another one.

The idea of conversion as a method of escaping the brutalities of the caste system was not a new one. Most Christian converts in late 19th-century Maharashtra were Mahars. Bhim, too, had thought about conversion and spoken about it as far back as 1927, during the Mahad conference where he said:

'We want equal rights in society. We will achieve them as far as possible while remaining within the Hindu fold or, if necessary by kicking away this worthless Hindu identity.'

But in the early 1930s, Bhim came to an important understanding of the religion he had been born into. Other religions, such as Christianity and Sikhism, spoke of how all human beings were equal before God, Hinduism said that God had divided human beings into four *varnas*. 'Hindus cannot destroy their caste system without destroying their religion,' he concluded.

An important conference was called at a place called Yeola in October 1935, and it was attended by about 10,000 Untouchables. Bhim addressed the crowd and asked them why so much energy, time and money had been spent trying to make the Hindu religion more just. Instead, he suggested, why not abandon Hinduism and seek another faith that would give them equal status?

'I solemnly assure you that I will not die a Hindu,' he said.

Those words would prove to be prophetic. At the conference, a resolution was passed to abandon Hinduism. The Untouchables pledged not to worship Hindu gods, to visit Hindu holy places and temples, or to to observe Hindu festivals and holidays.

Bhim's decision to renounce Hinduism created a massive uproar. Orthodox Hindus were worried that if the Untouchables converted to another religion, they would swell the numbers of that faith and Hinduism would be weakened, both demographically and electorally. Gandhi criticized Bhim for proposing such a mass conversion and argued that it would discourage reformers who had been working to abolish untouchability. Gandhi also said that religion was a spiritual matter, and one could scarcely change one's religion at will, as you might change a coat or a house.

However, the leaders of other minority groups were very happy with this new development. Muslim and Christian leaders made welcoming gestures towards Bhim in the hope that the Untouchables would convert to their religions. The Buddhists also made friendly overtures, but it appears that Bhim had not decided on Buddhism at that point. Instead, he explored the idea of conversion to Sikhism.

In November 1936, Bhim travelled to London to seek constitutional guarantees from the British for Untouchables converting to Sikhism. But by the end of 1937, Bhim had abandoned the idea. What changed his mind? For one, the British refused to extend constitutional concessions that were available to Sikhs in the Punjab to Sikh converts as well.

Additionally, the Sikh Dalits told Bhim of the injustices they had suffered at the hands of the Jats. Their accounts made Bhim realize that even Sikhism was not free of inequality. Besides, many Sikh political leaders were worried that with the influx of so many Untouchable converts, their own influence would become diminished. They were possibly relieved when Bhim gave up the idea of converting to Sikhism and did not try harder to woo him.

However, Bhim did not stop considering an alternative to Hinduism. His first efforts at abandoning Hinduism weren't successful, but they did demonstrate that the idea of mass conversion was a powerful political strategy. It could pressure caste Hindus to reform their religion or to risk losing large numbers of low-caste Hindus to conversion.

In a booklet titled *Annihilation of Caste*, Bhim argued that the Hindus did not practise caste because they were inhuman; they practised caste because they were deeply religious and their religion demanded it. The fault lay in Hinduism, he said, and to reform the religion, belief in the scriptures—the Shastras and the Vedas—had to be challenged.

There had been signs, early on, that Bhim was drawn to Buddhism. Bhim's first introduction to Buddhism came in the form of a biography of the Buddha, written by his old teacher K.A. Keluskar and gifted to him when he was just a boy. His young mind had been very affected by the life of Gautama Buddha and this manifested in different ways throughout his life. When he built himself a house in Mumbai in 1934, he called it Rajagriha, the name of the capital of the ancient Buddhist kings of Bihar. In 1948, he published *Untouchables*, in which he argued that the Untouchables were descendants of the Buddhists, who had been neglected after the bulk of Indian society crossed over to Hinduism. The first college opened by the People's Education Society founded by Bhim in the mid-1940s was called Siddharth College, named after the Buddha.

Buddhism was a religion that was more open to interpretation and reinterpretation than any other creed Bhim had come across so far. The Hindus have the Bhagvad Gita and the Muslims have the Koran, but while the Buddhists, too, have many sacred texts, they do not have a canonical text whose teachings they have to rigidly follow. In other words, Buddhism did not appear to be as unchangeable as Hinduism. There was no caste system among the Buddhists, and the Buddha taught that all human beings were one in the eyes of God.

Eventually, Buddhism came to exert such a powerful influence on Bhim that he was able to keep his promise to 'not die a Hindu'. It was in 1956, twenty years later, that Bhim officially converted to Buddhism. As the father of the Indian Constitution, he lobbied hard for the official recognition of Buddhism. He threw a great challenge to orthodox Hindus, and he demonstrated that conversion to

Buddhism was a viable method of social revolt and change. And although conversion to Buddhism did not bring about the social transformation that Bhim had dreamed of, he became a guru to his community by showing them a spiritual way out of centuries of oppression.

Is Dalit Buddhism the Navayana?

The word 'yana' means mode or method of spiritual practice. There are two traditionally recognized branches of Buddhism: Mahayana and Hinayana. Both are considered alternative paths to enlightenment. Navayana, or the new vehicle, is often used to refer to the Dalit Buddhist movement, because Buddhism enjoyed a major revival in the 1940s and 1950s, after Bhim explored it as an alternative religion for the Untouchables.

Perhaps, the term 'Navayana' derives from a press interview Bhim gave in 1956, in which he said: 'I will accept and follow the teachings of Buddha. I will keep my people away from the different opinions of Hinyan and Mahayan, two religious orders. Our Bouddha Dhamma is a new Bouddha Dhamma, Navayan.'

12   A New Party Is Born

The developments of the 1930s left Bhim very disillusioned about the future of the Untouchables who desperately needed a strong political presence if their voices were to be heard. With a view to giving his community this platform, in 1936, Bhim founded the Independent Labour Party (ILP).

As its name indicated, it was not a party confined to the Untouchables. This was a key dilemma that Bhim struggled to resolve. Should the Untouchables think of themselves as a separate group, or be more inclusive in nature? Bhim understood that he needed to widen his support, and his new party attempted to speak not just to the Untouchables, but also to the landless labourers in the villages and industrial workers in the cities.

The year 1936 was coming to a close and elections in eleven provinces—as mandated by the Government of India Act of 1935—were coming up fast. Every party was making frantic preparations to fight elections. Bhim's own party was a David to the Congress's Goliath. The Congress Party had men and money at its disposal and enjoyed the reputation of being a party of patriots. It was an all-India party and had members across the country, whereas Bhim's party was confined to the Bombay Province.

There were 175 seats up for grabs in the Bombay Legislative Assembly, but only fifteen seats were reserved for Untouchables. This election presented a unique challenge. A party that managed to capture all the seats in the Untouchable quota would still not be able to stand up to the might of the ruling party. In other words, there would be no effective opposition to the Congress if the ILP only had fifteen seats. And so, Bhim decided to set up some more candidates for the general seats and also supported a few independent candidates.

The Congress Party put up candidates in all provinces. But the Congress fought its hardest for one particular seat—the seat that Bhim contested himself in Bombay. Bhim was their most bitter enemy, their arch-rival, the challenger of their values and ideals. They could not bear the thought of losing to him.

Bitter as defeat was, Congress had to swallow it eventually. Bhim was elected with a resounding majority. Of the eighteen candidates put up by the ILP in the Bombay Province, fifteen were elected. The Congress shuddered at the idea of meeting Bhim head-on in the Assembly. They knew, without doubt that he would make a tough opponent. This wasn't the only victory to come Bhim's way. The Bombay High Court finally decided the long-drawn-out case over the Chavdar Tank in March 1937, in favour of the Depressed Classes.

Once elected, Bhim did not waste any time getting down to business. In September 1937, he proposed a bill to abolish the *vatan* system. Introduced by the British, a *vatan* was a fragment of land given to a Mahar as payment for services rendered to the village. The *vatan* was a bittersweet gift, because in its exchange, the Mahar had to slave day and night, often performing demeaning duties that no caste Hindu would stoop to.

His bill was met with stiff resistance and all sorts of excuses were made for why the bill could not be passed. It was impossible to put a money value on the customary duties performed by Mahar vatandars, the government argued. It is more likely that the government feared that paying Mahars for their services according to the market rate would take its toll on the treasury. In fact, the Mahar *vatan* system was not abolished until in 1959, after Independence.

At the same time, Bhim also proposed a bill to abolish the *khoti* system. Under this system, land tax was collected by the *khot*, typically an upper-caste Hindu, who served as middleman for the government. The Congress opposed this bill, too, arguing that they had already planned their own separate reforms of the *khoti* system. The reality was that the Congress was reluctant to annoy the Brahmin and Maratha property owners who dominated the party. As a result, the *khoti* system was not abolished until 1949.

Bhim was also eager to reach out to urban workers, and in 1935, he formed a trade union for the municipality workers of Bombay, the Bombay Municipal Kamgar Sangh, which grew from 800 members in 1937 to 1325 workers in 1938.

In 1938, Bhim protested against the Industrial Disputes Bill being considered in the Bombay Legislative Assembly because it made it illegal for an industrial labourer to go on strike. Calling it a 'bad, bloody and brutal' piece of legislation, Bhim argued that making a man serve against his will amounted to slavery.

The ILP and the Bombay Municipal Kamgar Sangh called for a one-day rally on 6 November 1938. After the rally, a huge procession, almost 80,000-strong, wound its way through the city. They planned to peacefully picket outside all mills and factories. Expecting that the procession would turn violent, the Government of Bombay called in 300 armed Reserve Police to man the mill gates. Bhim, in a lorry decorated with red flags, reminded the workers to stay peaceful. Almost all the textile mills and municipal workshops closed down that day. As a finale to the successful strike, another rally was held that evening and workers charged with a heady sense of victory burned an effigy of the bill.

In 1938, there was yet another occasion for Bhim to lock horns with the Congress Party. The Untouchables were to be renamed Harijans, or the children of God. Bhim argued that a mere change of name would not improve the conditions of the Untouchables. The term 'Harijan' annoyed Bhim because it assumed that Untouchables were the children of a Hindu god even though Hinduism had been nothing but cruel to the Untouchables.

Bhim proposed an amendment to reject this new name for the Untouchables, but the amendment was shot down and the term 'Harijans' was forced upon the Untouchables. It was an almost tragic irony that the Untouchables were not even given the right to decide what they should be called.

Why was there a need to liberate Mahars from the *vatan* system?

The *vatan* was a bittersweet gift, because the Mahar vatandar had to slave day and night for it. A vatandar had to perform services that were often demeaning in nature, services that no caste Hindu would stoop to perform. In addition to the land, a vatandar was paid a small pittance for his hard work.

Bhim wanted to abolish the *vatan* system so that Mahars could enjoy a new sense of self-respect and could explore other sources of livelihood. However, he argued, they should not be evicted from the land that had been given to them, but instead they should be allowed to occupy it as payment for their services. He wanted to transform them into property owners, and free them from their customary duties. His bill was nothing less than an overhaul of the traditional village economy.

What was wrong with the *khoti* system?

The *khoti* system was liable to be abused by the *khot*, who could keep a part of the revenue he collected. He often set himself up as a local gang-lord, bullying the tenants who lived on his land and forcing them to work for free.

13   The 1940s

In 1939, World War II broke out, drawing in more than 100 million people from thirty different countries. Germany invaded Poland, and in response, Great Britain and France declared war on Germany. Almost every country of the world was forced to pick sides between the Allies and the Axis in the worst conflict in human history.

India, as a British colony, was committed to the war by a proclamation of the British Viceroy. But Indians were divided on this issue. Some, like Bhim, supported the war effort because they believed that cooperation with the British would win them eventual freedom. Bhim also argued that if India did not support Britain, the country would only fall to new masters.

Others, like the Congress, were unhappy that the British government had involved India in the war effort without consulting Indian leaders. The Congress ministries introduced a war resolution in all the provincial assemblies. It declared that the British government had made India a participant in the war without consulting Indians. To protest this, the Congress resigned in all the provincial governments where it held power.

It was only in mid–1940, when the war looked grim for Britain and her allies, that Congress leaders did a volte-face. They abandoned Gandhi's leadership and decided to extend their cooperation to British war efforts. What they asked for in exchange was an assurance that a fully representative National Government would be formed at the centre. This came to be known as the Poona offer.

The Poona offer was rejected. In response, the Congress threw its support behind Gandhi again. In October 1940, Gandhi initiated the Civil Disobedience Movement, preaching that India should not take part in the war on the grounds of non-violence. Almost all Congress leaders were thrown into prison.

Later, in an interview to *The Times of India*, Bhim described Gandhi's rebellion as both irresponsible and insane. The barbarians were at the gates of India, he said, and this was no time to weaken the British. He called Gandhi an old man in a hurry.

Meanwhile, the British were beginning to recognize Bhim's growing stature as a political and economic thinker. In early 1941, he asked for and was granted expanded recruitment of Untouchables in the armed forces. He also successfully pushed for the reinstatement of the Mahar battalion in the Indian Army.

Later that year, Bhim was appointed to the Viceroy's Defence Advisory Committee. The aim of the committee was to involve Indian politicians in the war effort. In 1942, Bhim was nominated to the Viceroy's Executive Council, becoming the first Untouchable Hindu to hold this post.

It was once said that the sun never sets on the British Empire. What this means is that the British Empire was once so vast, the sun was always shining on some part of it. But the experience of fighting two world wars had turned Britain into a ghost of its former self. In 1942, British-held Singapore fell to Japan, and the British Empire reeled from the shock.

In March 1942, the British government hastily sent out a delegation led by Sir Stafford Cripps, a senior British politician, to end the political deadlock in India. The aim of the Cripps mission, as it came to be known, was to persuade Indian leaders to join Britain in the war for a promise of eventual independence for India. The Cripps proposal offered India dominion status and promised to form a constituent assembly after the war ended. The constituent assembly would draft the constitution.

However, the mission failed because the Congress was wary of Cripps' promises and wanted immediate self-government for India in return for war support. Gandhi described the Cripps proposal as a post-dated cheque. The Muslim League also rejected the Cripps proposal as it did not contain a definite guarantee in favour of the creation of Pakistan. Bhim, too, did not accept the Cripps proposal as there was no mention of representation for the Untouchables, and he feared that the Untouchables would be bound to Hindu rule forever.

Though the Cripps proposal did not find support, it brought about major changes in the Untouchable movement. During an interview with Bhim, Cripps asked him whether he represented the labouring classes or the Depressed Classes. The ILP was not a pure Scheduled Caste party, and the British were questioning how Bhim could call himself a leader of the Scheduled Castes without a specific scheduled caste organization behind him. As a result, Bhim decided to shut down the ILP, and at a conference in Nagpur in July 1942, the All-India Scheduled Caste Federation was formed.

The Scheduled Caste Federation took shape as a national party, something the ILP had not succeeded in doing. It brought together all the emerging leaders of Dalit movements all over the country. At the conference, the proposals of the Cripps mission were declared unacceptable. The Untouchables also said that no constitution would be acceptable to them unless it recognized the Scheduled Castes as being separate from the Hindus.

In August of the same year, the Congress launched the Quit India Movement. It was a response to Gandhi's call for immediate independence for India, and as a result, Congress leaders all over the country were arrested. The arrests prompted mass uprisings that were ruthlessly clamped down on by the British all over the country. India was plunged into chaos for two years.

In all the fervour of the Quit India Movement, Bhim took a different stand. He reasoned that non-cooperation with the British would be playing into the hands of fascists.

Bhim was right to have concerns about the spread of fascism which was a radical authoritarian political ideology born in Italy under the dictatorship of Benito

Mussolini. The fascists are united in their belief in war and political violence as a method to rejuvenate the nation. During World War II, there were many fascist stirrings in Europe, particularly the regime of Adolf Hitler in Nazi Germany. Japan, which had allied with Italy and Germany, was also heading in a fascist direction since the 1930s. The Japanese army was on the brink of invading India, and if the British were weakened, India would fall to Japan.

It was perhaps this tendency of Bhim's, to stand apart from the crowd, to think differently from the others, that often earned him the undeserved title of a traitor. He was not afraid of following his convictions, even when he could not find others to agree with him.

In spite of his support of the British, Bhim's expectations were to be largely disappointed. In 1942, the Depressed Classes were still terribly underrepresented in government. There were only two Untouchables in the National Assembly and only one—Bhim himself—in the Executive Council. Out of 1056 members of the Indian Civil Service, only one was an Untouchable.

Bhim appealed to the British to treat Untouchables as a minority, just like the Muslims, Sikhs or Parsis, and to reserve a quota for them in administrative jobs because business and industry were inaccessible sectors for them. In the field of education, there were only about 500 Untouchable graduates in 1940. Bhim proposed granting more scholarships to Untouchable students, but his suggestions were ignored.

In June 1945, Lord Archibald Wavell came to India to try to negotiate what came to be known as the Wavell Plan, an agreement for the self-rule of India. Congress leaders were released from jail and a conference was called in Shimla. Wavell began discussions with Gandhi, Nehru and Muhammad Ali Jinnah but projected an indifferent attitude toward the Untouchables. This made it quite clear that the politics of the day still mainly revolved around the Muslim League and the Congress. In the days ahead, Bhim would have to focus all his energy on ensuring that the Dalits were not left out.

The Wavell talks stalled, however, over differences between Jinnah and the Congress. Lord Wavell returned to London in August 1945 to consult others on the problem. He returned to India in September and announced general elections that year to test the support enjoyed by different political parties.

All the parties contested elections. This was the first election in which the Scheduled Caste Federation was fighting as a national party of the Depressed Classes. The Congress stood with the Quit India slogan. Jinnah entered with the Pakistan or Perish slogan. The Scheduled Caste Federation had no funds or election machinery. The party was badly defeated in the elections. At least one thing was now clear—to secure a future for the Untouchables, Bhim would have to make amends with the Congress Party.

In March 1946, Cripps visited India again as part of a new cabinet mission. The mission met with the Congress, the Muslim League and with princely leaders.

The Scheduled Caste Federation's failure at the elections made Bhim's position as the undisputed leader of the Untouchables a shaky one. Bhim was interviewed, but other leaders of the Untouchables were given a hearing, too.

There were a number of ideas that Bhim put forward at this time. He asked the mission to make a constitutional provision for separate electorates for the Depressed Classes. He also asked for adequate representation for the Depressed Classes in the Legislature and the Executive, both provincial and central, and in public services. He appealed for an educational allowance to be earmarked for the Untouchables so that more students from the community would have access to education.

On 16 May 1946, the mission declared its decision to form an Indian union with three groups of provinces which would be broken up into the following groups: Madras, UP, Central Provinces, Bombay, Bihar and Orissa; Punjab, Sindh, Northwest Frontier Province, Baluchistan; Assam and Bengal. It recommended an undivided India and the Muslim League's clamour for a separate Pakistan was ignored.

The mission also recognized India's right to withdraw from the Commonwealth. A constituent assembly would be formed and an interim government would be set up. This interim government would be made up of Indians with minimal interference from the Viceroy. The union government would only have power with regard to Finance, Foreign Affairs, Defence and Communication, or Union subjects. The provinces would have all subjects other than Union subjects, and the princely states would have all subjects, including Union subjects. There was no mention of any of the demands that Bhim had put forth.

Now, as a new government was to be formed by the winning parties, the Viceroy disbanded his Cabinet. Bhim left Delhi and returned to Bombay. He found himself facing a political stalemate, and this weighed down his spirits. He sensed that this was his last chance to secure the rights and interests of his community.

At a Poona conference in July the same year, he called for the Untouchables to launch a satyagraha against the mission's proposals. His satyagraha was criticized bitterly by the Congress, who accused Bhim of being frustrated because his party had lost the elections. But Bhim was not being a sore loser. Instead, he argued that India's Untouchables had a right to demand a blueprint from the Congress regarding their rights and interests after independence.

Meanwhile, members were elected by the provincial legislatures for the new Constituent Assembly. The Congress elected its representatives, not so much on the basis of whether they had the knowledge required to draft a constitution but as a reward for suffering imprisonment in the Independence struggle and being loyal party members. Having lost elections, Bhim had no one to back him in the Bombay assembly, but he managed to be elected from the Bengal assembly.

In June, the names of the members of the Interim Ministry were announced. Bhim was not on the list.

Yet again, the Dalits were poorly represented, this time in the newly formed Cabinet. This was a bitter setback for Bhim and his party. In a last-ditch effort to win the rights of the Untouchables, Bhim went to London to sway British politicians in his favour.

The visit was a futile one. It appeared that the only way forward was for Bhim to seek assurances from the Constituent Assembly that the rights of Untouchables would be safeguarded. He would have to work side-by-side with his old arch-enemy, the Congress Party. This would test all his diplomatic skills in the months to come.

Who were the Allies and the Axis?

The Axis powers, primarily made up of Germany, Japan and Italy, fought World War II against the Allies. The Allies entered World War II either because they had been invaded, or because they feared imminent invasion, or because they feared that the Axis powers would control the world if they went unchallenged. The Allies included Great Britain, France, the United States, China, Australia, New Zealand and India.

What is a constituent assembly?

A constituent assembly is formed to write a new constitution or to adopt an existing one. The Constituent Assembly of India was elected to draft the Constitution of India. Its members went on to form India's first parliament.

What was the Quit India Movement?

The Quit India Movement was a civil disobedience movement launched by Gandhi in August 1942. Also known as the August Movement, it was meant to force the British to grant immediate independence to India in return for Indian cooperation during World War II. In his stirring speech to the people, Gandhi used the slogan 'Do or Die'. But less than twenty-four hours after his speech, the movement was repressed. Gandhi and other Congress leaders were thrown in jail. Processions and assemblies were banned. But there were many popular riots and demonstrations all over the country in support of the movement.

14 📝 The New Manu

Marginalized by the British, Bhim was politically astute enough to recognize that the time had come to make friends. His exclusion from the interim ministry had left him isolated, and with the partition of Bengal, he had lost his seat in the Constituent Assembly. Bhim needed Congress support to reclaim his seat in the Constituent Assembly, without which he would not be able to influence the Constitution of independent India. It was a delicate moment, and Bhim, every bit a politician, needed to make amends with the Congress. The reconciliation occurred in the Constituent Assembly in December 1946.

Although the Muslim League had boycotted the Constituent Assembly, the assembly met as scheduled. Nehru had moved a resolution to declare India an independent sovereign republic. The resolution was going to be passed when Bhim stood up and advised the Constituent Assembly to postpone a vote until the Muslim League joined the Assembly.

In a passionate speech, Bhim said, 'I have not the slightest hesitation that we shall in some form be a united people.'

After years of opposing the Congress, his talk of unity and oneness thrilled the hearts of all the

Congressmen present, and won them over. The harmony between Bhim and the Congress continued to build and grow through 1947.

In March 1947, he presented to the Constituent Assembly his own version of an ideal constitution. In it, he demanded separate electorates for the Untouchables as well as the redistribution of state land so that the Untouchables could be settled in separate villages. Bhim's suggestion for separate electorates met with great resistance from the Congress majority. Separate electorates would divide the community, argued the Congress. Congressmen did not want to betray Gandhi, who had gone on a fast unto death in Poona in 1932 to oppose the principle of separate electorates.

Also, these were the early days post-Partition. India had recently been torn into two countries. There had been bloody riots and violence, with a heavy human cost for both the Hindus and Muslims. The Congress felt that the root cause of Partition was the granting of separate electorates to the Muslims decades earlier. By granting separate electorates to the Dalits, they feared that history would repeat itself. In such an environment, Bhim abandoned his demand for separate electorates, but it was only a tactical retreat, because there was a bigger battle to win.

On 29 April 1947, a momentous day in the history of the Untouchables, the Constituent Assembly agreed to abolish untouchability and made its practice a punishable crime. It was no longer legal to practise discrimination based on caste, race and gender.

Finally, it seemed that there was light at the end of the tunnel. Here was new hope for the Untouchables that they would finally be integrated into Indian society. But while the world press lauded this day as one of freedom of the Untouchables, the credit for attaining this freedom went to the Congress Party, and to Gandhi. No foreign publication mentioned Bhim's name.

On 3 August 1947, Nehru appointed him law minister in the first government of independent India. In both the Constituent Assembly as well as in government, Bhim lobbied hard for greater rights for the Untouchables.

Three weeks after being appointed law minister, Bhim was also appointed chairman of the constitutional drafting committee. In his able hands, a radical new constitution was taking shape and he needed support to push his ideas through. This was his hour of glory and the focus of all his attention from 1947 to 1950. It was certainly no time to alienate the Congress.

The drafting committee was composed of some of India's most learned people. Although Bhim was at the helm, it is only fair to say that all the members of the drafting committee contributed valuable thoughts and ideas to the constitution we have today. They did not draft the primary text of the Constitution, because the Constitution drew a lot from the 1935 Government of India Act. But this does not mean their job was an easy one.

The committee read and studied the constitutions of many other countries, absorbing what was best from each of them. They knocked the primary text of the Constitution into shape on the basis of articles submitted by specialized subcommittees, which were then submitted to the Constituent Assembly for approval.

In the Assembly, the drafts were read and discussed, and Bhim played a leading role in guiding the debate and gently nudging it forward. Bhim was also one of the few members of the Constituent Assembly who belonged to more than one of the fifteen other committees besides the drafting committee. This way, he could closely follow all the debates on vital constitutional articles. It was a long painstaking process, and the debate over the Constitution continued for three whole years!

Bhim drew heavily upon the Western political ideas that had influenced him during his years studying abroad. He championed the creation of a liberal democracy. What did this mean? The Constitution, Bhim argued, was a mechanism for regulating the work of the various organs of the state. It was not supposed to tie down people to live in a predetermined society that could not be changed. It was supposed to allow people the liberty to decide what sort of society they wished to live in.

In the Constitution, he enshrined the ideas that he had spent his entire life struggling for: liberty, equality, fraternity and justice. Having sat outside the classroom, having been forbidden from touching water, he knew how important equality and liberty were to a person's quality of life.

It was under Bhim's leadership that the principle of reservation was written into the Constitution so that the rights of women, children and backward classes would be protected. 'If all communities are to be brought to the level of equality, then the only remedy is to adopt the principle of inequality and to give favoured treatment to those who are below the level,' he said.

He was very concerned that India would transform itself into a political democracy, but not a social and economic one. 'In politics we will have equality and in social and economic life we will have inequality,' he said. To ensure socio-economic change, Bhim outlined the Directive Principles of our Constitution. A concept borrowed from the Irish Constitution, the principles cannot be legally enforced. Instead, they are meant to be guidelines to attain socio-economic change. They are the very spirit of our Constitution.

Some Directive Principles were political ideals that were ahead of their time. For example, Bhim imagined a uniform civil code throughout India, but the idea was too radical and would never get passed to become a part of the main Constitution. Instead, it found its way into the Directive Principles as something that India should aspire to in the future. Other Directive Principles were Gandhian ideas that Bhim found too conservative to work into the Constitution, such as the promotion of cottage industries in rural areas, or the prohibition of cow slaughter. Instead, these ideas were cleverly embodied in the Directive Principles.

Bhim's work on the Constitution is a matter of great pride for Dalits across India. It earned him the title of father of the Indian Constitution, the modern Manu, which is a little ironic because Bhim had rejected and burned the old laws of Manu, many years ago, during the Mahad satyagraha.

All the freedoms that we take for granted today found permanence in Bhim's Constitution. On 4 November 1948, it was a historic moment when the draft Constitution of India was presented in the Parliament by a former Untouchable! And on 26 November 1949, the Constituent Assembly, in the name of the people of India, adopted the Constitution with its 395 articles and eight schedules.

That moment gave Bhim the image we see today, on statues of Bhim that stand all over the country: blue suit, tie, horn-rimmed spectacles, hair carefully combed, and the Constitution of India in one hand.

How does the Constitution protect the Untouchables and promote their interests?

The Constitution provides a three-pronged legal framework to protect the rights of the Untouchables and it also provides for the setting up of a National Scheduled Castes Commission to ensure that these laws are properly implemented.

1. Laws to protect Untouchables from discrimination and cruelty, and laws to punish such acts.
2. Laws for affirmative action so that Untouchables get preferential treatment with regard to access to jobs or to education.

3. Laws that provide the resources required to bridge the gap between the Untouchables and the rest of society.

What is reservation and why is it so controversial?

Affirmative action was a term that was first used in the United States. It refers to policies that give equal opportunity to a particular group of people who have been historically discriminated against, on grounds of race, gender, colour or religion, to name a few. Reservation is one form of affirmative action.

In India, certain seats in educational institutions and government jobs are reserved for underprivileged communities. The Constitution of India divides them into Scheduled Tribes, Scheduled Castes and Other Backward Classes. The system of reserving seats for backward communities goes back to pre-Independence times. In the first official example of reservation, Shahu Maharaj introduced reservation for backward classes in his princely state of Kolhapur.

Reservation is a controversial issue because many people from the higher social classes think that it goes against the basic right to equality, but it is meant to be a counter to centuries of oppression.

15   Independence, Now What?

With Independence, the political struggle against the British had ended. But for Bhim, the struggle continued, the far-more important struggle for social reform. Despite Independence, India was still a country plagued by inequality and injustice in many forms. The Untouchables were yet to become equal members of Indian society. Women were still to win rights of inheritance. They could be forced to live with their husbands and had no right to divorce, and nor could they control money or open their own bank accounts.

A spate of new laws aimed at reforming regressive Hindu traditions had marked the century before Independence. Sati, or the burning of a widow on her husband's funeral pyre, was banned in 1829. The Hindu Women's Right to Property Act was introduced in 1937. The British decided to club all these reformed Hindu laws into one code, which was known as the Hindu Code Bill. The bill was introduced in the legislature in April 1947, but in all the turmoil of Independence and Partition, the text of the bill could not be discussed. In 1948, Nehru nominated Bhim as the head of a sub-committee charged with drafting a new Hindu Code Bill.

Bhim was now at the zenith of his popularity. He was the architect of the Indian Constitution, and now he could vindicate himself in front of all the people who had named him pro-British and anti-Hindu. His birthday in April 1950 was celebrated on a nationwide scale and attended by many prominent dignitaries. Now, the drafting of the Hindu Code Bill gave him, a Mahar, the golden opportunity to reform the basic framework of Hindu society. It was a chance that he could not pass up!

Little did Bhim foresee that his efforts to get the Hindu Code Bill passed would rake up huge controversies in a newly independent India. He poured all his energies into drafting this bill. An entire room in his home was filled with all the reading material he would need for the job. He studied the scriptures closely, holding lengthy discussions with jurists and religious scholars alike. His progressive ideas of equality and justice shaped the bill. He knew that the bill would be one of the cornerstones for a modern-thinking India. Essential principles were written in, such as equality between men and women on the question of property inheritance, and making monogamous marriages the rule, to ensure that a Hindu husband could not take more than one wife. Divorces would have to be justified, said the bill. A man would now have to present good reasons for wanting to end his marriage. The bill aimed at giving women more power and equality in their marriages.

The new Hindu Code Bill was submitted on 16 August 1948. It created a very emotionally charged atmosphere across the country and polarized opinion. Many Congress leaders were too traditional and set in their ways to accept these new ideas and so railed against them. Hindu marriage was sacred, they argued, and dissolving a marriage would ruin society. Women who supported the bill were attacked for being too aggressive.

The debate dragged on and the bill came up for final reading only in September 1951. The new marriage system, Bhim said in a speech, was not an imitation of the West, but based on the values of liberty, equality and fraternity found in the Constitution. The sacred marriage that the orthodox Hindus spoke of, Bhim said, was nothing more than slavery for the woman.

His logic and arguments fell on deaf ears. As a result, the bill was watered down in the legislature and finally buried. In disappointment and frustration, Bhim resigned as law minister. In his letter of resignation, he wrote that by ignoring social reforms, Indian leaders were trying 'to build a palace on a dung heap'.

Newly independent India was moving forward without resolving its glaring social inequities, which was a matter of grave concern to Bhim. What sort of country would the Dalits inherit? Would they have any voice in independent India?

With the electoral defeat of his party, the Scheduled Caste Federation, Bhim saw the need to transform the leadership of the Depressed Classes. He envisioned a new party based on the principles of liberty, equality and fraternity. He called it the Republican Party, after the party of American president Abraham Lincoln, whose leadership had brought an end to slavery in America. While most of its members were Untouchables, the party was now meant to represent all oppressed sections of society.

Meanwhile, Bhim's health was failing. He was suffering from rheumatism and diabetes. He had not been sleeping well, and excruciating pain in both his legs kept him up. He felt keenly the need for a companion to look after him in his old age. He felt that he wanted to be with an educated lady who could practice medicine, and so in April 1948, Bhim married Dr Sharda Kabir, his physician. Keeping with Maharashtrian customs, she took a new name, Savita. It is also interesting to note that she was a Brahmin!

By 1955, Bhim was having trouble moving about the house on his own. His eyesight was fast failing and he also had trouble breathing, needing to be given oxygen a few times a week. He kept these details a secret because he did not want to frighten his followers with the thought that he might be dying, but he had lost weight and his clothes hung upon him.

Despite his poor health, Bhim never stopped reading and writing. He would sit at his desk for hours, working on books about Buddhism and Hinduism. He was very drawn to Buddhism, believing that it was the only religion that could emancipate the Dalits. In a speech that was broadcast on British radio, he explained why he was drawn to Buddhism. It was the only religion that preached three important principles of *prajna* (understanding), *karuna* (love) and *samata* (equality).

Bhim had once taken a vow: 'Even though I am a Hindu born, I will not die a Hindu.'

Twenty years later, on 14 October 1956, he kept his vow by converting to Buddhism in Nagpur. It was the day of the Hindu festival of Dussehra, and it was a historic occasion. Thousands of his followers came to Nagpur on buses and trains, even trekking hundreds of miles on foot to catch a glimpse of their leader converting to Buddhism. They came dressed in white, some of them bearing ochre flags, the colour of Buddhism.

The Burmese Bhikku Mahasthaveer Chandramani was invited to carry out the ritual. Bhim and his wife, Savita, were the first to convert, which they did under a canopy in front of the crowd. Bhim then asked the thousands of Untouchables awaiting conversion to stand up. He administered the Buddhist vows to them. Nearly three lakh Untouchables embraced Buddhism with him that day. This is possibly the largest single mass conversion in human history.

As part of the Constituent Assembly, Bhim pushed hard for Buddha Jayanti, the birth anniversary of the Buddha, to become an official holiday. Constitutional provisions were made to promote the study of Pali, the language of the earliest Buddhist scriptures. Between 1947 and 1950, he was also involved in the adoption of many Buddhist symbols that are an unquestioned part of our daily lives today: the chakra on the Indian flag, the lions of Ashoka, and an inscription of a Buddhist proverb on the pediment of Rashtrapati Bhavan, the residence of the president of India.

And in this way, Bhim became a guru to his community, yet unlike most gurus, he was honest enough to warn them that converting to Buddhism would not be a cure-all. Under any new religion, they would have to fight for liberty and equality. He was also pragmatic enough to warn his followers against worshipping any leader and elevating him to the status of a deity. He warned, presciently, '. . . Bhakti, or what may be called the path of devotion or hero worship, plays a part in [Indian] politics unequalled [elsewhere] . . .'

By converting, Untouchables did not need to suffer for a moment longer, the indignity of being low-born within the Hindu fold. After being rejected by the Hindus for centuries, they, in turn, rejected the Hindus, and their leader, Bhim, had found a spiritual refuge for them in Buddhism, whose teachings had been all but forgotten for the last 1200 years.

What is Bhim's place in Indian Buddhism today?

Despite warning his community against hero worship, Bhim is worshipped as a bodhisattva today, an embodiment of the Buddha, in Maharashtra as well as among the Jatavs of northern India. Many converts worship only Bhim and Buddha, and their birthdays alone are observed as religious holidays.

16 ✎ Bhim's Legacy

On 6 December 1956, Bhim's lifelong struggle against the injustice of the social systems of India came to an end, two months after his conversion. He died in his sleep at his home in Delhi at the age of sixty-five. Bhim had always worried that his ill health would cut short his life before he had completed his mission of bringing freedom to the Dalits. At the end of his life, untouchability had been abolished, seats had been reserved in Parliament for Dalits, and millions of people could imagine a more equal world. It was a task large enough to daunt a giant, and Bhim had fulfilled it.

His funeral procession on 7 December was one of the largest in the history of Bombay. Over half a million people gathered, crying, even fainting in grief, and they showered petals and garlands on his body. He was cremated by the seashore in Bombay. Interestingly, one lakh people embraced Buddhism at the funeral pyre of their leader. Buddhists rose in number from 2500 in 1951 to 2.5 million in 1961! In Maharashtra, the palanquin of the village goddess, which was typically kept and looked after by the Mahars of every village, was returned to upper-caste Hindus. There was tension, often violent outbreaks, too, as Mahars shook off their ritual obligations.

After his death, Bhim was worshipped as a bodhisattva, an embodiment of the Buddha, clad in a saffron robe (even though being worshipped would have been the last thing he wanted). His birthday was declared a national holiday, and today, many converts observe only two religious holidays—Bhim's birthday and the Buddha's.

Bhim's was a short life, and yet a most remarkable one. He rose up from dust, from being treated worse than an animal to becoming the father of the Indian Constitution. He spent his boyhood being shunned constantly, friendless and alone at school. He starved through university life, saving every penny for his family back home and to buy books.

It was not easy at any point to fight his way forward without a family fortune behind him, and yet he did. He turned his hardships into an opportunity to become stronger and to fight harder. He was unafraid of opposition, of thinking differently from the crowd, and of speaking his mind.

Bhim always led by example. He showed his followers, through the way he lived his own life, that education and hard work alone held the key to their liberation. The Untouchables had been a demoralized, helpless group of people, but Bhim taught them to stop waiting for help to come from the outside, and to rely upon themselves instead. This idea was a revolutionary one for a people who had always been told that their lot in life was preordained and that they had no control over it.

You can change your lot, Bhim said, but do not flock to temples hoping for justice to come to you in heaven. There is justice to be found on earth if you can fight for it. This idea gave them a new courage and a sense of self-respect that they had never known before.

The Untouchables had been treated like outsiders in their own country, but Bhim ensured that they got constitutional rights, something they could never have even dreamt of a hundred years ago. By his relentless campaigning against the caste system, both in India and abroad, he gave untouchability a global face and made it a burning issue. It became part of national and international debate.

Bhim, in his brief lifetime, managed to acquire several university degrees at the finest schools in the world, to edit newspapers, to write books, to become the principal of a law college, to lead mass movements, to address public conferences, and to work on committees involved with the making of the Indian nation. It was as though he sensed very early on that he had a lot to achieve and that time would always be running out for him.

He was an intellectual giant, and perhaps if the plight of the Untouchables had not pushed him into politics, he would have been a scholar. Books were his best friends, and yet he never read for amusement. He read to learn. 'What instructs me amuses me,' he once said. His library was his refuge, and no one was allowed to touch a single book without his permission. He finally parted with his library to donate it to Siddharth College, but continued to purchase new books.

He was a true Renaissance man, a person who excelled in many different areas of inquiry. Books were not his only weakness. He had a penchant for fountain pens of all kinds. He enjoyed well-tailored clothes, and loved pedigree dogs. As an adult, he took up both painting and playing the violin because he believed that every man should love music and art. His hobbies, be it reading or music, spoke of his softer side. But in his political career, not many people saw this side of Bhim, though. He was often described as a British bulldog and Sarojini Naidu once called him Mussolini. There is perhaps no one who had escaped his sharp tongue and unforgiving sarcasm, especially if those rebukes were deserved. He was truthful to the point of being harsh.

Perhaps his childhood experiences steeled him for a life in which popularity did not come easily. He had many enemies and detractors. But he had the self-confidence to know that future generations of Hindus would come to understand his services to the nation. He did not let the fear of disapproval stop him from doing the right thing.

He once said: 'I am the most hated man in Hindu India.'

Though he was hated by orthodox Hindus and labelled as a destroyer of Hinduism, historians now realize the crucial role Bhim played in reorganizing Hindu society. Far from being a traitor, he played an important role in revitalizing Hinduism, reviving it by challenging everything that was unjust and unfair within it. In fact, he brought about a renaissance of Hinduism by provoking the Hindus to rethink some of the basic tenets of their religion.

He was as outspoken about his ideas of nation-building. He possessed great foresight, and his warnings about the future of India ring so true today. In a speech before the Constituent Assembly, he cautioned his fellow-legislators against the use of non-constitutional methods of protest, such as civil disobedience and satyagraha, because they were essentially anarchic in nature.

He railed against the Indian tendency to engage in hero worship. He was afraid that the people of India would lay their liberties at the feet of someone they worshipped, or entrust them with extraordinary, limitless powers. He also underlined the importance of creating not just a political democracy, but also a social and economic one.

Although he is mainly remembered for his work to uplift the Untouchables of India, Bhim had other significant achievements that go unremarked upon. As a Labour member of the Viceroy's Executive Council, he passed the Indian Trade Unions (Amendment) Bill, making it compulsory for a trade union to be recognized in every business enterprise. He fought for minimum wage and safe working conditions, for laws to regulate female employment and for miners' conditions to be improved. He also concerned himself with formulating policies to promote irrigation and electric power. He emphasized the need for a power grid system, one that we use even today.

It is a true contradiction that while Dalits across India erect countless statues of Bhim, our history books only refer to his work on the Indian Constitution or his stature as a leader of the Untouchables. It is a terrible failing that Bhim is not counted among the legions of great Indian freedom fighters. The most educated Indians are often unaware of his life and its impact on society. Everyone speaks of Gandhi's social reforms and Nehru's secular vision, when it was probably Bhim who understood these ideas more deeply than anyone else.

There was no mention of him in official speeches for decades after Independence, and it was only in 1990 that he was awarded a Bharat Ratna posthumously, India's highest honour. In the same year, his portrait was put up in Parliament, next to the portraits of other Indian greats. What a great omission for it not to have been done earlier!

Bhim drew flak for being too sympathetic of the West, and for opposing the Mahatma so vehemently. Perhaps he is forgotten because he did not align himself with the Congress Party. In a letter to Sardar Vallabhbhai Patel, he wrote that he was a nationalist without being a Congressman.

This observation of his points to a grave error in our history books, where the Indian Independence movement is often considered synonymous with the Congress Party. Patriots and freedom fighters, as Bhim's example clearly shows, can also be found outside it. Our history books also make the mistake of assuming that the only Indian struggle of note in the first half of the 20th century was the struggle for independence from the British.

Bhim was a freedom fighter of the truest kind, not merely dreaming of setting India free from British rule, but of transforming India into a country where freedom holds meaning for everyone. While Gandhi led fellow-Indians in a struggle against discrimination in South Africa, Bhim led a battle, too, against prejudice within his own country. By securing equality for his community, he was creating a more equal world for us all.

'Turn in any direction you like, caste is the monster that crosses your path,' he wrote. The story of Bhim's life is as relevant today, when we are still to rid ourselves of the monster of caste. Bhim's journey is as eventful and as eye-opening as the train ride that began it all, where a little boy discovered, for the first time, the terrible agony of being born Untouchable.

Does untouchability exist only in India?

It doesn't. The Dalits exist as a group in Pakistan, Nepal and Bangladesh as well. The Burakumin of Japan, the Al-Akhdam of Yemen, the Baekjeong of Korea and the Midgan of Somalia are also groups that have been traditionally persecuted.

The Burakumin were given the 'impure' work in feudal Japan—they worked as slaughterers, leather tanners, executioners and undertakers. Although the feudal caste system has been abolished, the Burakumin still face discrimination.

The Al-Akhdam of Yemen (Akhdam means 'servant') live on the fringes of society and are given menial jobs to do. Similarly, the Baekjeong (Baekjeong means 'common

---

people') of Korea were the untouchable outcastes in traditional Korean society, and there were strict rules about how they could behave and dress. The Midgan or Madhibaan of Somalia were traditionally hunters. These days, they are engaged in leatherwork and shoemaking, but they are still looked down upon by the rest of Somali society because of the work they do.

TRIVIA
TREASURY

Turn the pages to discover more fascinating facts and tantalizing tidbits of history about this legendary life and his world.

INDIA UNDER BRITISH RULE

Company rule or Company Raj refers to that period in history when India was directly ruled by the British East India Company. There isn't a single agreed date for the beginning of Company Raj in India. It could be said to have started in 1757, after the Battle of Plassey, when the Nawab of Bengal surrendered his dominions to the Company.

It could also be said to have begun in 1765, when the Company was granted Diwani, or the right to collect revenue in Bengal and Bihar. Additionally, 1772 was the year when the Company established a capital in Calcutta and appointed its first Governor-General, Warren Hastings, and became directly involved with governance.

Following the revolt of 1857, Company rule ended and the British government directly took over the administration of India and ushered in the British Raj. The India Office was created in 1858. This was a British government department in charge of the administration of India and other territories, which included the modern-day nations of India, Pakistan, Bangladesh and Burma, and parts of Southeast and

Central Asia, the Middle East and the east coast of Africa.

The post of Secretary of State for India, or India Secretary, was created the same year. The Secretary of State was a British Cabinet member responsible for the governance of India and he was the political head of the India office. The India Office and the office of the Secretary of State were both abolished in 1947 when the Partition of India led to the creation of two separate countries, the Union of India and the Dominion of Pakistan.

The office of Governor-General of India was a much older one. Before 1858, the Governor-General was selected by the East India Company's Court of Directors. But after 1858, the territories governed by the East India Company came under the direct control of the British government. The Governor-General was now appointed by the British monarch on the advice of the British government, and the Secretary of State for India was meant to advise him on the exercise of his powers.

The title of Governor-General of India was first created in 1773, but it was only in 1833 that the Governor-General was given complete authority over British India. In 1858, when the British Raj began, the Governor-General of India was head of the Central Government of India. This included eight major provinces: Burma, Bengal, Bombay, Madras, United Provinces, Central Provinces and Berar, Punjab and Assam. There were also a few minor provinces, such as the North-West Frontier Province and the Andaman and Nicobar Islands.

Apart from these provinces, there were hundreds of native states or princely states that were not ruled directly by the British government. These states recognized the ultimate authority of the Crown, but they also enjoyed internal autonomy. For the rulers of these native states, the Governor-General of India represented the monarch, and so his title was altered to Viceroy and Governor-General of India.

The Governor-General was always advised by a Council, although its composition changed over the years. At first, it was composed of four counsellors elected by the East India Company's Court of Directors. Later, in 1919, an Indian Legislature, comprising a Council of State and a Legislative Assembly, took over the legislative functions of the Viceroy's Council.

The title of Viceroy was abandoned when India and Pakistan gained Independence in 1947, but the title of Governor-General continued till both countries became republics, India in 1950 and Pakistan in 1956.

THE WORLD IN BHIM'S TIME

- **1853**: The first commercial passenger-train service in India left Bombay's Bori Bunder for Thane.
- **1892**: Homer Plessy is arrested for sitting on the whites-only train-car in Louisiana.

- **1894**: The first Sino-Japanese War is declared between the Qing Empire of China and the Empire of Japan.
- **1895**: The Treaty of Shimonoseki is signed between China and Japan, ending the first Sino-Japanese War; Wilhelm Röntgen discovers a type of electromagnetic radiation later known as X-rays; Auguste and Louis Lumière display their first motion picture film in Paris.
- **1897**: Queen Victoria celebrates her Diamond Jubilee.
- **1898**: The Spanish-American War begins; Marie and Pierre Curie discover radium.
- **1901**: The Commonwealth of Australia is formed; Queen Victoria dies.
- **1902**: Robert Falcon Scott, Ernest Shackleton and Edward Wilson's Discovery Expedition is hailed as a landmark in British exploration of the Antarctic, but it does not reach the South Pole.
- **1903**: Edward VII is proclaimed Emperor of India.
- **1904**: The Russo-Japanese War begins. It ends in 1905 with Japan's victory, establishing Japan as a world power.
- **1905**: The Russian Revolution starts with police firing on a crowd of peaceful demonstrators, giving rise to the Russian Constitution, limited monarchy and the establishment of the Duma in 1906.
- **1910**: George V becomes king upon the death of his father, Edward VII.
- **1911**: The Delhi Durbar is held to mark the coronation of King George V and Queen Mary as Emperor and Empress of India, and the shift of the capital of the British Raj from Calcutta to Delhi.

- **1912**: The Republic of China is established; *The Titanic*, the unsinkable ship, strikes an iceberg in the northern Atlantic and 1500 lives are lost.
- **1913**: *Raja Harishchandra*, the first full–length Indian feature film, is released, marking the beginning of the Indian film industry.
  Mohandas Gandhi is arrested while leading a march of Indian miners in South Africa.
- **1914**: Austrian Archduke Franz Ferdinand is assassinated, triggering World War I.
- **1918**: The Spanish Flu becomes pandemic; over thirty million people die in the following six months (almost twice as many died during World War I).
- **1919**: Benito Mussolini founds Fascist movement in Italy. The Treaty of Versailles is signed, formally ending World War I.
- **1921**: Adolf Hitler becomes Fuhrer of the Nazi Party; Albert Einstein is awarded the Nobel Prize in Physics for his work on the photoelectric effect.
- **1922**: Benito Mussolini becomes youngest premier in Italian history.
- **1925**: Adolf Hitler publishes *Mein Kampf.*
- **1926**: Francisco Franco becomes General of Spain.
- **1927**: Charles Lindbergh makes the first solo nonstop transatlantic flight, from New York City to Paris.
- **1930**: The Great Depression, the longest, most widespread and deepest depression of the 20th century, hits worldwide.
- **1932**: The Battle of Shanghai marks the beginning of the Second Sino–Japanese war.

- **1934**: Adolf Hitler becomes dictator of Germany.
- **1936**: King George V dies. His eldest son succeeds, becoming Edward VIII.
- **1938**: German troops invade and occupy Austria.
- **1939**: Albert Einstein signs a letter addressed to President Franklin Roosevelt about developing the atomic bomb, leading to the creation of the Manhattan Project; Germany invades Poland. The United Kingdom, France, New Zealand and Australia declare war on Germany.
- **1940**: Germany invades Denmark, Norway, France, the Netherlands, Belgium and Luxembourg; Winston Churchill becomes Prime Minister of the United Kingdom; Auschwitz-Birkenau, the largest of the Nazi concentration camps, opens in occupied Poland. Between 1940 and 1945, around 1.1 million people will be killed here.
- **1941**: Germany invades Yugoslavia and Greece; German forces besiege Leningrad; the Japanese Navy attacks Pearl Harbour, drawing the United States into World War II.
- **1945**: Two atomic bombs, code-named Little Boy and Fat Man, are dropped on the Japanese cities of Hiroshima and Nagasaki respectively. A week later, Emperor Hirohito of Japan announces Japan's surrender on the radio.
- **1947**: The Cold War begins when U.S. President Harry Truman implements the Truman Doctrine to fight the spread of Communism; India becomes independent from British rule; The Indo-Pakistan

War, also known as the First Kashmir War, breaks out.

- **1950**: The Korean War begins between Democratic People's Republic of Korea (North Korea) and Republic of Korea (South Korea) over the control of the Korean Peninsula.
- **1951**: Libya gains independence from colonial rule.
- **1952**: George VI of the United Kingdom dies after a long illness. He is succeeded by his daughter, Princess Elizabeth, who is crowned Elizabeth II.
- **1953**: President Truman announces that the United States has developed a hydrogen bomb.
- **1954**: The First Indochina War ends. The Algerian War begins, with Algeria fighting for independence from French colonialism.
- **1956**: Sudan becomes independent from British occupation, and Morocco and Tunisia become independent from France. Oct 29—The Suez Crisis begins.

BHIM'S LIFE: WHAT HAPPENED AND WHEN

- **14 April 1891:** Bhim is born at Mhow (Madhya Pradesh), the fourteenth child of Subedar Ramji Sakpal and Bhimabai.
- **1896:** Bhim's mother dies.

- **1900:** Bhim is enrolled at the Government Middle School in Satara.
- **1904:** Bhim attends Elphinstone High School in Bombay.
- **1907:** Bhim passes the Matriculation Examinations.
- **1908:** Bhim is admitted to Elphinstone College, Bombay.
- **1912:** Bhim passes the BA exams from University of Bombay. Bhim's first son, Yashwant, is born.
- **Feb 1913:** Bhim's father dies.
- **July 1913:** Bhim goes to Columbia University.
- **1915:** Receives an MA degree from Columbia University.
- **June 1916:** Leaves Columbia University after completing work for a PhD, and joins the London School of Economics and Political Science. He also trains for Law at Gray's Inn.
- **1917:** Returns to India after his scholarship is terminated by Baroda State.
  Appointed as Military Secretary to the Maharaja of Baroda, but leaves Baroda soon after.
- **1918:** Accepts a professor's job at Sydenham College of Commerce and Economics, Bombay.
- **1919:** Appears before the Southborough Commission.
- **Jan 1920:** Starts a Marathi newspaper, *Mooknayak*.
- **Mar 1920:** Presides over a Depressed Classes conference at Kolhapur.
- **July 1920:** Bhim leaves India to resume his studies in London.
- **June 1921:** London University accepts Bhim's thesis

Provincial Decentralisation of Imperial Finance in British India and awards him an MSc. (Econ) degree.

- **1922:** Bhim is called to the Bar.
- **1922–23:** Spends some time reading economics at the University of Bonn in Germany.
- **1923:** Bhim returns to India. His thesis *The Problem of the Rupee—Its origin and its solution* is accepted for a DSc. (Econ) degree.
- **1924:** Starts law practice in the Bombay High Court. Founds the Bahishkrit Hitkarini Sabha.
- **1926:** Nominated member of the Bombay Legislative Council.
- **Mar 1927:** Starts Mahad Satyagraha to secure the Untouchables' right to drink water from the Chavdar Tank.
- **Apr 1927:** Starts and edits a bimonthly Marathi paper, *Bahiskrit Bharat*.
- **June 1927:** Awarded PhD degree from Columbia University.
- **Dec 1927:** Second conference at Mahad.
- **1928:** Introduces the Vatan Bill in the Bombay Legislative Council. Becomes professor of Government Law College, Bombay.
- **1930–32:** Represents India's Untouchables at the Round Table Conferences.
- **Sept 1932:** Signs the Poona Pact to save Gandhi's life.
- **1934:** Leaves his home in Parel and moves residence to 'Rajagriha' at Dadar. This was done to accommodate his ever-increasing collection of books.

- **May 1935:** His wife, Ramabai, dies.
- **June 1935:** Appointed Principal of Government Law College, Bombay.
- **Oct 1935:** At the Yeola Conference in Nasik, he urges his community to leave Hinduism and embrace another religion. He declares: 'I solemnly assure you that I will not die a Hindu.'
- **Aug 1936:** Bhim founds the Independent Labour Party.
- **Feb 1937:** The first General Elections are held. Bhim is elected member of the Bombay Legislative Assembly.
- **March 1937:** The Chavdar Tank case is decided in favour of the Depressed Classes.
- **Sept 1937:** Bhim introduces two bills in the Bombay Assembly, one to abolish the Mahar Watan and the other to abolish the *khoti* system.
- **May 1938:** Bhim resigns as principal of Government Law College, Bombay.
- **Nov 1938:** The industrial workers strike.
- **Oct 1939:** Bhim meets Jawaharlal Nehru for the first time.
- **1941:** Bhim fights to recruit Mahars in the army. The Mahar Battallion is formed. Bhim is appointed to the Defence Advisory Committee.
- **June 1942:** Bhim becomes the first Untouchable to join the Viceroy's Executive Council.
- **July 1942:** Bhim founds the All-India Scheduled Caste Federation in Nagpur.
- **1946:** Bhim is elected member of the Constituent Assembly of India.

- **April 1947:** Article 17 for the abolition of untouchability is moved by Sardar Vallabhbhai Patel in the Constituent Assembly.
- **Aug 1947:** India gets independence. Bhim joins Nehru's cabinet as the first Law Minister of independent India. The Constituent Assembly appoints him to the drafting committee.
- **Feb 1948:** Bhim completes the draft Constitution.
- **Apr 1948:** Bhim marries Dr Sharda Kabir.
- **Nov 1948:** Bhim presents the draft Constitution to the Constituent Assembly.
- **Nov 1949:** The Constituent Assembly adopts the Constitution.
- **Sept 1951:** The Hindu Code Bill comes up for a final reading. Bhim resigns from the Nehru cabinet because it fails to support the bill.
- **Jan 1952:** Bhim faces defeat in the first Lok Sabha elections.
- **March 1952:** Bhim enters Parliament as a member of the Rajya Sabha, representing Bombay.
- **June 1952:** Columbia University confers on Bhim the honorary Degree of LL.D. (Doctorate of Law), in its bi-centennial celebrations held in New York.
- **Oct 1956:** Bhim embraces Buddhism at a historic ceremony in Nagpur, witnessed by thousands of followers. He declares that he will dissolve the Scheduled Caste Federation and establish the Republican Party.
- **6 Dec 1956:** Dies at his residence in New Delhi.
- **7 Dec 1956:** Ambedkar is cremated at Dadar

Chowpatty, which is now known as Chaitya Bhoomi Dadar (Bombay).

BHIM'S LEGACY

In India

- 14 April, or Bhim's birthday, is observed as a national holiday. It is known as Bhim Jayanti or Ambedkar Jayanti.
- 19 March is observed by Bhim's followers as Independence Day because it marks the day their struggle first began at Mahad.
- Buddha Jayanti, or the birth anniversary of Lord Buddha, is now a national holiday.
- The Ashoka Chakra, a Buddhist symbol, is recognized as our national symbol.
- A Buddhist aphorism is inscribed at Rashtrapati Bhavan.
- An image of Buddha, installed by Bhim, stands in the Buddha Vihara at Dehu Road, near Pune.
- In every city in India, there is possibly a hospital, an educational institution or a street named after Bhim.
- Numerous statues of Bhim can be found all over the country, including some notable ones like the one standing outside the Rajya Sabha in Delhi, or the one at Oval Maidan in Mumbai.

- In 2000, Jabbar Patel made a film called *Dr Babasaheb Ambedkar*, starring Mammootty in the lead role. He won the National Film Award for Best Actor. The film also won the National Film Award for Best Feature Film in English.

Abroad

The European Romas or Gypsies are as alienated from mainstream society as the Dalits in India. They describe themselves as the Untouchables of Europe. Inspired by Ambedkar, they have set up the Jai Bhim network. The network runs educational and social organizations for the Gypsies. A large number of them have also converted to Buddhism. As Ambedkar did as well, the Jai Bhim network emphasizes self-help. Bhim's message to 'Educate, Agitate, Organize' finds an echo with them, and they look up to Bhim as their hero.

Ambedkar in Literature

Scores of books have been written on the life of Bhim, his influence on Buddhism, his work on the Constitution and his struggle against untouchability. (To begin with, look at our Reading List.)

Bhim himself authored several books in his lifetime. Here are a few titles:

1. *Annihilation of Caste* (1936)
2. *Thoughts on Pakistan* (1946)
3. *Buddha and His Dhamma* (1957)

4. *What Congress and Gandhi Have Done to the Untouchables* (1945)
5. *Who Were the Shudras?* (1946)

THE GROWTH OF DALIT LITERATURE

Bhim didn't just inspire India's Untouchables to fight for their freedom, he also gave rise to a new genre of Dalit literature. Though stories about the experience of being Dalit have been around as far back as the 11th century, the term 'Dalit literature' came into use only after 1958, when the first conference of the Maharashtra Dalit Sahitya Sangha was held, in Mumbai.

It was Jyotiba Phule who first voiced the idea of a separate genre of literature that could express the Dalit experience. Bhim was supposed to preside over the first conference for Dalit literature, but the conference was postponed with his untimely death on 6 December 1956.

Bhim's struggle to free India's Untouchables inspired a group of Dalit writers and poets to express the 'Dalit voice'. In the years following Bhim's death, there was an explosion of writing by Dalits—poetry, fiction and autobiographies. Dalit literature emerged as a steady voice, first in Marathi and then in other languages like Hindi, Kannada, Tamil and Telegu. It is often likened to

African–American literature because it deals with similar issues of injustice and segregation.

Baburao Bagul was the pioneer of Marathi Dalit literature, although the most memorable name in Marathi Dalit literature remains that of Namdeo Dhasal, who died only recently, on 15 Jan 2014. In 1992, the Ambedkari Sahitya Parishad was formed in Wardha, Maharashtra, to provide a new platform for Dalit literature. The next year, the parishad made moves to reconceptualize Dalit literature as 'Ambedkari Sahitya' after its hero.

What makes Dalit writing so powerful? Perhaps it is the frankness with which it deals with the pain of being an Untouchable. Perhaps it is its depth and maturity. Either ways, Dalit writing has earned a place as one of the distinct forms of Indian writing.

BOOKS TO READ

Here are some books you can read if you want to find out more about Bhim and his ideas:

1. *Dr. Babasaheb Ambedkar* by Dhananjay Keer (Popular Prakashan, 1954)
2. *Ambedkar: Towards an Enlightened India* by Gail Omvedt (Penguin, 2004)

3. *Dr. Ambedkar and Untouchability* by Christophe Jaffrelot (Permanent Black, 2005)
4. *We, the Children of India: The Preamble to Our Constitution* by Leila Seth (Puffin, 2010)
5. *Makers of Modern India* by Ramachandra Guha (Penguin, 2011)
6. There are several books written by Bhim himself, including *Waiting for a Visa*, which is a collection of his reminiscences. This is available on the Internet.
7. To read some remarkable examples of Dalit writing, look for poetry by Namdeo Dhasal, such as *Golpitha*, or read Arjun Dangle's *Poisoned Bread: Translations from Modern Marathi Dalit Literature.*